Poverty and Distributional Impact of Economic Policies and External Shocks

Göttinger Studien zur Entwicklungsökonomik
Göttingen Studies in Development Economics

Herausgegeben von/Edited by Hermann Sautter und/and Stephan Klasen

Bd./Vol. 18

PETER LANG

Frankfurt am Main · Berlin · Bern · Bruxelles · New York · Oxford · Wien

Jann Lay

Poverty and Distributional Impact of Economic Policies and External Shocks

Three Case Studies from Latin America Combining Macro and Micro Approaches

PETER LANG
Europäischer Verlag der Wissenschaften

Bibliographic Information published by the Deutsche Nationalbibliothek
The Deutsche Nationalbibliothek lists this publication in the Deutsche Nationalbibliografie; detailed bibliographic data is available in the internet at <http://www.d-nb.de>.

Zugl.: Göttingen, Univ., Diss., 2006

Gratefully acknowledging the support of the Ibero-Amerika-Institut für Wirschaftsforschung, Göttingen.

Cover illustration by Rolf Schinke

D 7
ISSN 1439-3395
ISBN-13: 978-3-631-56559-9

© Peter Lang GmbH
Europäischer Verlag der Wissenschaften
Frankfurt am Main 2007
All rights reserved.

Printed in Germany 1 2 3 4 5　7

www.peterlang.de

Acknowledgements

I am grateful to my supervisor Jun.-Prof. Dr. Michael Grimm for his academic support and his patience. I am indebted to the Kiel Institute for the World Economy that provided an inspiring work environment as well as financial support in the past few years.

I wish to thank my colleagues in Kiel, Rainer Thiele and Manfred Wiebelt, who co-authored the chapter on Bolivia, as well as Maurizio Bussolo and Dominique van der Mensbrugghe at The World Bank, who co-authored the chapter on Brazil, for the endless but productive discussions and the many hours spent together "crunching" numbers.

Special thanks go to Anne-Sophie Robilliard (and again to Maurizio, Manfred, and Rainer) for introducing me to the methods used in this dissertation. Many other colleagues and friends have provided ideas, comments, and technical as well as moral support: Christiane Gebühr, Olivier Godart, Robert Kappel, Gernot Klepper, Rolf Langhammer, Matthias Lücke, Toman Omar Mahmoud, Cornelius Patscha, Susan Steiner, Saju Thundiyil, and the team of the development economics research group at the University of Göttingen led by Prof. Stephan Klasen, Ph.D. Encouragement came from many other people as well, in particular from my family.

Contents

List of Figures

List of Tables

1. General introduction and main findings

The extent to which economic growth reduces poverty has always been a central issue in development economics. Obviously, the extent depends on the distribution of the benefits of growth.[1] Already by the late 1950s, it became apparent that growth in "underdeveloped countries" did not trickle down to the population at large, but was instead accompanied by massive underemployment and unemployment. This "employment problem" implied that growth did not necessarily translate into poverty reduction, but rather to increasing inequalities between those who remained poor and those who were lucky enough to find employment in modern urban sectors. This was consistent with the Kuznets' (1955) hypothesis of an inverted U-shaped relationship between inequality and development, according to which inequality would tend to increase in the early stages of development. Kuznets (1955) admits that his often cited paper is "perhaps 5 percent empirical information and 95 percent speculation, some of it possibly tainted by wishful thinking."

Despite these observations, it took until the 1970s and the work of Adelman and Morris (1973) and Chenery et al. (1974) until the question of income distribution within a country explicitly entered the debate. Adelman and Morris (1973) even reached the conclusion that "development is accompanied by an absolute as well as relative decline in the average income of the very poor", although they were challenged by Cline (1975) and Lal (1976) that this finding was not borne out by their data. Lal (1976) harshly criticized these studies and argued that the "concern with distributional issues amongst the international agencies and American development economists marks more their acknowledgement of *their* neglect of what a number of Third World governments and many development economists have for a long time recognized to be a major area of concern". This assessment certainly contained some truth, but these studies had a significant influence on the research agenda. Lal (1976) went on to conclude that these studies "may perhaps do indirect damage to the prospects of the poor by not emphasizing enough that efficient growth, which raises the demand for labor is probably the single most important means available for alleviating poverty in the Third World". The latter statement illustrates the ideological nature of the discourse between those who "emphasized" growth and others who "emphasized" distribution. This is mainly owed to the fact that the debate of the 1970s still rested, to stick to Kuznets'

---

1   This introduction focuses on the discourse in development economics with regard to and the empirics of *the impact of economic growth and economic policies on the distribution of income*, and hence on poverty. For reviews of the theories of development and distribution see Cline (1975) and Kanbur (2000). This focus also implies that we do not consider the reverse causal relationship from inequality to growth. See Atkinson and Bourguignon (2000), Aghion et al. (1999) for literature reviews and the 2006 World Development report (World Bank 2005a) for recent empirical insights.

wording, on very little empirical information, a lot of speculation, and possibly even more on wishful thinking.

The emphasis on distributional and poverty issues however was relatively short-lived. With the arrival of the debt crisis in the early 1980s, the focus of both development policy and research shifted towards structural adjustment to current and capital account imbalances. As this went along with the arrival of conservative governments in OECD countries, the view that development and poverty reduction could best be reached through economic growth and free markets dominated. In this environment, little research effort was dedicated to resolve the issues raised by earlier empirical studies on the relationship between the distribution of income and economic development and it took until the early 1990s to put the issue back on the agenda.[2]

In the late 1980s, concerns were raised that the costs of structural adjustment programs, which were implemented in most developing economies, were disproportionately borne by the poor (Adelman and Robinson 1989).[3] In the course of the 1990s, this concern was replaced by the worries, in particular voiced by non-governmental organizations, that the benefits of globalization would be concentrated on the rich in the developing world. In the policy arena, the adoption of the Millennium Development Goals in 2000, which put poverty reduction at the centre of development policies, created demand for detailed micro datasets necessary to monitor progress on the poverty reduction goals. Possibly, the major reason why income distribution was back on the research agenda is related to data availability. Investigators could rely on more data of much better quality, in particular on household survey data, thereby dramatically reducing the degree of speculation contained in earlier studies.[4]

In recent years, a burgeoning literature has significantly improved our understanding of the relationship between growth, poverty, and inequality. Today, it is widely acknowledged that on average growth is distribution-neutral and hence reduces poverty (Ravallion and Chen 2003, Dollar and Kraay 2002). In that sense, "growth *is* good for the poor" (Dollar and Kraay 2002). Ravallion (2001a) however suggests that one needs to look "beyond averages", as the impact of economic growth on poverty differs substantially across countries. In addition, he notes that this impact can also vary among the poor in a given country. That it is indeed worthwhile to look "beyond averages" is confirmed by many country studies that in recent years have cast light on the very different income distribution

---

2   Exceptions include a major research project by The World Bank initiated in 1985, the results of which are summarized in Fields (1989), and some country studies e.g. on Malaysia by Anand (1983).

3   The UNICEF study "Adjustment with a human face" that examines the poverty impact of structural adjustment with a focus on children and other vulnerable groups received a lot of attention at that time. See Cornia, Jolly, and Stewart (1987).

4   See Deaton (1997 and 2003) on data issues.

dynamics during growth both across countries and across time.[5] These dynamics vary case by case, which almost makes it impossible to draw any general conclusions from this literature, not even by region or confined to a specific time-period. The only exception is the increase in inequality throughout the late 1980s and 1990s. Inequality measured by the Gini-coefficient, increased in 6 out of 7 country cases presented in Bourguignon et al. (2005a) covering the 1980s to the mid-1990s and in 8 out of 14 cases in the OPPG[6] project covering the 1990s.

The differences in country experiences of course raise the question of why is this so. It turns out that even more diversity can be found when one attempts to identify the drivers of distributional change. The studies in Bourguignon et al. (2005a) employ microsimulation methods[7] to decompose historical changes in income distributions into "fundamental sources": (1) Changes in the resources at a household's disposal, including human capital accumulated through education, as well as socio-demographic changes, such as changes in the area of residence, age structure, and households composition (endowment or population effects), (2) changes in market remuneration of the factors of production (price effects), and (3) changes in the occupational structure of the population, in terms of labor market participation and formal or informal sector of employment (occupational effects).[8] The main general lesson from the country studies is that observed changes in the distribution of income result from a number of sources, which may offset or reinforce each other. Since country experiences differ considerably, only few common patterns can be identified. One of these patterns is that price effects, i.e. changes in returns to education, were typically inequality increasing. Some

5   See Christiaensen, Demery, and Paternostro (2003) for a review of a number of Sub-Saharan cases, the country studies on pro-poor growth in the 1990s in World Bank (2005b) and Grimm, Klasen, and McKay (2006), and the collection of East Asian and Latin American experiences in Bourguignon, Ferreira, and Lustig (2005a).

6   "Operationalizing Pro-Poor Growth" was a joint research program undertaken by The World Bank and the French, German, and British donor agencies. The results can be found in World Bank (2005b) and Grimm, Klasen, and McKay (2006).

7   In the tradition of Oaxaca (1973) and Blinder (1973), poverty and distributional changes between two (or more) points in time are decomposed using two (or more) cross-sections of households. This is achieved via simulating counterfactual distributions on the basis of household income generation models that will be described in more detail below. See Bourguignon, Fournier and Gurgand (2001) and Grimm (2005) for further applications of this technique.

8   It should be noted that this empirical operationalization of distributional drivers implicitly reflects the insights from the grand long-term theories of development and distribution from Lewis (1954) and Kuznets (1955) with their focus on intersectoral movements out of a traditional subsistence into a modern enclave sector to recent models originating from endogenous growth theory where externalities, such as parent-to-child human capital or economy-wide technological externalities, drive accumulation, growth and inequality dynamics (Kanbur 2000). It also mirrors short-to-medium term distributional adjustments to external shocks and policy changes that can be explained in a simple neoclassical trade model with fixed factor supplies.

conditional findings include the distributional effect of increasing female labor market participation that is found to be very positive when mainly females from poorer households entered the labor market. Increasing informality generally contributes to increases in inequality and is shown to very strong impoverishing effects on the poor in Brazil. Educational expansion improves the income distribution in some cases, but it can also be inequality increasing in the presence of earnings that are highly convex in years of schooling despite improving the distribution of education.

These findings illustrate the wealth of insights into the microeconomics of income distribution obtained by this type of decomposition analysis. Yet, such an approach leaves many questions open. First and foremost, these questions concern the factors that explain changes in what Bourguignon et al. (2005b) call the "fundamental" sources of distributional change. In other words, which are the factors that explain the increase in wage inequality in many countries, the increase in female labor market participation, increases/decreases in informality, the patterns of educational expansion, and socio-demographic changes? Possible explanatory factors can be grouped into phenomena related to socio-economic development in general, such as demographic changes and human capital accumulation, external shocks, and economic policies. In particular external shocks and policies related to globalization, such as increased trade and capital flows, the related pattern of technological change, and external liberalization, have recently received a lot of attention as possible reasons for the observed increase in inequality in many countries. The empirical assessment of these "fundamental causes" of distributional change is by no means trivial. It implies to analyze the poverty and distributional impact of specific external shocks, economic policies, or other relevant events, rather than analyzing the reduced-form relationship between changes in the distribution of income and economic growth. Such analyses are extremely policy-relevant, in particular when development policies are geared towards poverty reduction.

The chapters in this dissertation therefore address the short to medium run poverty and distributional impact of economic policy changes and external shocks for three Latin American countries.[9] More specifically, chapter 2 examines the impact of trade liberalization in Colombia in the early 1990s. Chapter 3 looks at the poverty and distributional implications of the gas boom in Bolivia. While these two chapters "ex-post" analyze past experiences, the third chapter attempts to assess "ex-ante" the possible effects of multilateral trade liberalization on poverty and the distribution of income in Brazil.

The country case studies included in this dissertation hence analyse the "micro" impact of "macro" events, which raises the question of the appropriate methodology to do so. In the short to medium run, macro policies as well as external shocks affect household incomes and consumption primarily through two channels; (1) through changes in returns to factors of production, in particular to

---

9   The short-to-medium run corresponds to 5 to 15 years.

labor, and in employment, and (2) through changes in relative goods prices. The empirical challenge now lies in linking the policy or external shock to these variables in a first step, in order to assess their impact on household welfare, i.e. the distribution of income and poverty, in a second step. In some cases, where a clear link between the shock and household welfare exists, this can be achieved relatively easily. Tax or price reforms, for example, directly affect real household income. Therefore, the distributional impact of such reforms can be evaluated relatively simply on the basis of household survey data.[10]

In most instances, however the analysis is complicated by the fact that there is no direct link between the shock and real household income. Another complication arises from general equilibrium effects that are ignored in the former approach. As a result, most analyses of the poverty and distributional impact of policies and external shocks have turned to Computable General Equilibrium (CGE) models. CGE models based on Social Accounting Matrices (SAM) provide a coherent analytical framework for understanding the complex mechanism through which economic policies and shocks affect household income distribution. Most CGE models applied to evaluate distributional impacts in developing countries are extended neoclassical models that incorporate important structural characteristics of these countries by assuming (a) limited substitution elasticities in various economic relationships and (b) various markets not to work properly.[11] They can be used for ex-ante assessment as well as for ex-post analysis in order to disentangle the effects of different shocks.[12]

CGE models for distributional analysis incorporate different representative household groups representing "classes" defined by area of residence (rural vs. urban), skill level (unskilled vs. skilled), socio-political factors (organized vs. unorganized workforce), or power and wealth (factor endowments, wealth, tenancy of land). In terms of distributional outcomes, the main defining features of

---

10 See Sahn and Younger (2002) for a short introduction into this approach. Often, such analyses do not account for behavioral responses, but this shortcoming could be remedied by estimating an appropriate empirical model that could be used to simulate behavioral change.

11 See Robinson (1989). Taking into account these structural characteristics was emphasized by the "structuralist" tradition of CGE modelling (see e.g. Taylor 1990). Only some "macro-structuralist" (Robinson 1989) features, such as markup-pricing and Keynesian multiplier effects did not make it into mainstream CGE modelling. The IFPRI (International Food and Policy Research Institute) standard model (Löfgren et al. 2002) in the tradition of Dervis et al. (1982) represents this current mainstream. Similar models have been applied to a number of countries. See Wiebelt (1996) for a detailed description of such a model for Malaysia.

12 The first big wave of studies using applied CGE models was motivated by the concern about the poverty and distributional impact of structural adjustment programs. A series of country studies undertaken by the OCED Development Centre tried to assess the impact of actual and (hypothetical) alternative structural adjustment packages on the poor (Bourguignon, de Melo, and Morrisson 1991). Sahn et al. (1997) contains a number of country studies from Sub-Saharan Africa.

these household groups in most CGE model applications are differences in their factor endowments and hence the incomes they receive. Possibly, household groups also differ in labor supply, consumption, and savings behavior. When a shock is applied to a CGE model, sectoral production changes, as do resource reallocations, factor and goods prices, as well as real income and consumption of the respective household groups. To translate the changes in real incomes of the respective household groups into poverty and distributional outcomes, one needs to specify the within-group income distributions. Two approaches have been proposed in the literature (Löfgren et al. 2002). The first, in the tradition of Adelman and Robinson (1978), is to fit (or to estimate) parametric distributions for each household group, e.g. the log-normal distribution that fits empirical income distributions reasonably well. This implies to categorize households in different groups according to the main sources of income or to other important socioeconomic characteristics of the head of the household. The change in mean real income of the respective household groups is applied to this within-group distribution, which is "shifted" accordingly. The within-group distributions are finally summed to give the overall income distribution. The second approach uses disaggregated household survey data, classifies households according to the CGE model household groups, and directly applies the changes in real household group income from the CGE to the survey. The calculation of poverty and inequality changes is then straightforward. This approach is also referred to as micro-accounting.[13]

The representative household group assumption implies that income distribution variations only result from changes between household groups, given that within household groups the variance is fixed.[14] Yet, recent empirical findings on distributional change indicate that changes within the typical representative household groups of CGE models account for an important share of overall distributional change.[15] At first sight, an obvious way out of this problem would be to increase the number of household groups, or even to incorporate all households from representative household surveys. The latter has been done e.g. by Harrison et al. (2000) in an assessment of Russia's accession to the World Trade Organization (WTO).[16] They find the differences in price effects between a model with 10 representative household groups and a model with 55 000 households to be negligible. This finding is not too surprising, as the failure of CGE models to capture some of the distributional dynamics is not grounded in the failure to account for household heterogeneity in terms of factor endowments and/or consumption patterns. The problem is rooted in the fact that CGE models do not account for decisions taken at the individual level. These individual decisions, for

---

13 See Lay, Thiele, and Wiebelt (2006) for an application.
14 For a detailed discussion of the problems of the representative household group assumption see Bourguignon, Robilliard and Robinson (2005).
15 See again the findings in Bourguignon et al. (2005a) and similar studies cited above.
16 Cockburn (2006) is another CGE application that incorporates all households from a survey.

example entry into the labor market, falling into unemployment or switching between sectors or occupations, are important drivers of distributional change. In other words, the CGE model treats the factor endowments of a household or household group as fixed (although these endowments may grow at an exogenous rate) and fails to represent individual decisions that may alter these endowments dramatically. Of course, CGE models can be extended to include, e.g. unemployment and/or endogenous labor supply. Yet, in order to capture the income distribution implications, decisions would have to taken by "real" individual household members. This implies to introduce individual "fixed effects" into the model and requires the estimation of structural labor market models (Bourguignon et al. 2005b).

Two approaches have been proposed to overcome these shortcomings of applied CGE models. First, individual behavior can be fully integrated into CGE models. There have been attempts to build such fully integrated models (Cogneau 2001, Cogneau and Robilliard 2001), but the results are mixed. In particular the formidable identification problems in estimating the structural labor market equations cast doubts on the robustness of this approach. Second, traditional CGE models have been sequentially linked to microsimulation models based on household income generation models that are estimated from household survey data. Using this approach, a pioneering study by Robilliard et al. (2002) examines the poverty and distributional effects of the Asian crisis. A comparison of the results to those obtained under the representative household group assumption reveals the superiority of using a microsimulation model. In the sequential approach, a shock is first simulated in the CGE model and then the microsimulation adjusts micro data so that values for its aggregate variables (wages and employment) are consistent with the CGE macro equilibrium. The "degree of consistency" between the macro and the micro model however differs between applications of the approach, but in a narrow sense a sequential model is confined to be inconsistent both theoretically and empirically. Theoretically, the changes, e.g. in wages and employment are driven by relative price changes, whereas the microsimulation typically only features a reduced-form representation of labor market behavior where prices do not appear as explanatory variables. Empirically, problems arise from the large differences in national accounts and household data, in particular with regard to labor value added, although some authors, e.g. Robilliard et al. (2002), manipulate survey weights to reach "empirical consistency". Yet if the analyst were able to reach complete theoretical and empirical consistency between the micro and the macro model, why not build an integrated model anyway.

The strength of the sequential approach lies in the combination of a structural macro model that allows tracing the transmission channels from macro shocks to prices and quantity changes relevant to distributional outcomes and a microsimulation model that provides a detailed account of the household income generation process. The microsimulation model used by Robilliard et al. (2002) follows Bourguignon, Fournier, and Gurgand (2001) and is similar to the one used in the country studies in Bourguignon et al. (2005a). In this model, household income is defined as the aggregation of earnings of individual household members, earnings from joint household activities and non-labor income, such as transfers or capital income. The econometric specification underlying the income generation process is composed of two types of equations, those describing occupational choices of the household members and earnings/profit equations. Household members typically choose between inactivity, wage employment and participation in a joint household activity, depending on individual and household characteristics. Decisions by household members are modeled sequentially, i.e. the household head's choice and related earnings enter the decision function of other household members, whereby the simultaneity of occupational choices within a household is taken into account. Of course, simulating poverty and distributional changes based on this type of household income generation models is not without shortcomings. Typically, the behavioral equations, e.g. those governing occupational choices, are estimated from cross-sectional data. It is hence assumed that the observed variation in behavior between individuals is used to simulate behavioral change of (other) individuals in time.[17] Yet, even if panel data was available, constant parameters would have to assumed for the simulation period, which apparently becomes an increasingly problematic assumption the longer time horizon of the analysis.

Two of the three country-studies in this dissertation, Bolivia and Brazil, use the sequential methodology that links a CGE and a microsimulation model – despite its imperfections. Both the CGE and the microsimulation model are adapted to the investigated shock as well as to the structural characteristics of the country in question. The studies explore the advantages of this innovative approach, but also hint at its shortcomings and suggest possible areas for improvements. The Colombia study uses a methodology that is similar in spirit. Counterfactual income distributions are generated using a household income generation model that is shocked by changes in earnings, employment, and relative goods prices. Yet, instead of using a CGE model to construct the counterfactual changes in these distributional drivers, we rely on other studies and additional descriptive analyses to identify the changes that can be related to the trade liberalization shock.

The issues addressed in the three following chapters are highly relevant and hotly debated in the Latin America context, but also beyond this sub-continent. Most Latin American countries are known for their very unequal income distributions and even the middle-income countries including Brazil and Colombia therefore exhibit relatively high levels of poverty. In such an environment, the evaluation of the poverty and distributional impact of policies and external shocks is key for the design of socially sustainable (and politically feasible) economic policies. In the case of external shocks, such knowledge can be important to

---

17   Although this assumption seems to be very restrictive, it can be plausibly made e.g. in
     the context of occupational choices, which are explained mainly by individual
     educational attainment, age, and household composition variables.

cushion possible adverse distributional and poverty effects. Economists have developed adequate tools for informing policy-makers ex-ante, i.e. before decisions are taken. The Brazil study contained in this dissertation is one example of such an ex-ante policy evaluation. Of course, much can be learned from looking at past experiences, which is what the other two chapters do.

The biggest "external" shock that has hit developing countries undoubtedly is globalization. As an integration process, it encompasses increased trade and capital flows as well as technology transfer. Eventually, globalization and increased interdependence in world markets are triggered by technological change and both domestic and multilateral policies, in particular trade and capital account liberalization. Hence, globalization has many facets.

The chapters in this dissertation shed light on the role of some of these facets in explaining distributional change. Whether trade liberalization, which is dealt with in chapters 2 and 3, is good for the poor and whether it increases inequality has been a major concern of many observers of developing countries.[18] The resource boom examined in the chapter on Bolivia may not be directly related to globalization, but the study's current relevance for many other developing countries stems from the fact that the globalization-related economic rise of China and India has fuelled world demand for commodities that are often exported by poor countries.

The remainder of this introduction shortly summarizes the main findings and major methodological features of the country studies. The following chapter examines the impact of trade liberalization in the early 1990s on income distribution and poverty in urban Colombia. It first analyzes the effects on the urban labor market, i.e. on labor earnings and employment, and relative goods price changes. Using a microsimulation model of the type described above, the chapter then analyzes how these changes have shaped the distribution of income and how they ultimately affect poverty outcomes. Increasing informality is found to have rather small effects, although very poor groups are affected disproportionately. The increase in the unskilled-skilled wage gap however has major negative distributional implications and lowers considerably the poverty reduction potential of growth. The relative price shifts for consumer goods have an unexpectedly strong positive distributional impact. Finally, the analysis demonstrates that two factors related to a non-tradable boom, increasing female labor market participation as well as an increase in informal profits, have played an important role in cushioning the possible adverse labor market effects of trade liberalization, in particular for the very poor.

The Bolivian chapter addresses the question of whether the gas boom of the 1990s has bypassed large parts of the poor population, thereby leading to increasing inequalities in an already unequal society. The chapter examines the

---

18 See Winters et al. (2004) for a very comprehensive review of the empirical evidence on trade and poverty. Some recent evidence with a focus on Latin America can be found in Harrison (2005).

transmission channels through which the large resource inflows related to the gas boom, both initial foreign investment in the sector and the subsequent export earnings, as well as large public transfer programs affect the distribution of income. These transfers may well be interpreted as a means of redistributing resource rents. The CGE model explicitly models the gas sector and takes into account its enclave character. The focus of the analysis is on the second round labor market impacts of Dutch disease type effects, in particular on shifts between formal and informal employment and changes in relative factor prices. The microsimulation model is specified accordingly. The simulation results suggest that the gas boom induces a combination of unequalizing and equalizing forces, which tend to offset each other. As net distributional change is limited, growth generated by the boom reduces poverty despite increasing informality.

For the Brazilian case, the next chapter intends to evaluate the poverty effects of possible trade liberalization outcomes of the Doha round in the medium run.[19] This implies to assess the poverty impact of a Doha Round (and a Full Liberalization) counterfactual scenario against a scenario that incorporates some of the main features of medium run structural change. The chapter thus examines whether the effects of trade liberalization, in particular on poverty and the distribution of income, are still prominent in the medium run. The main poverty-relevant transmission channels incorporated in the simulation exercise are changes real factor prices and changes in the sectoral composition of the workforce, focusing on employment movements between agricultural and non-agricultural sectors. Structural change is driven by changing consumption patterns, differentials in productivity growth rates across sectors, educational upgrading of the workforce, and, finally, the trade shocks. The methodology combines again a sequentially dynamic CGE model with a microsimulation model that takes into account educational expansion on the micro level. The analysis suggests that the economic effects of the Doha round, even of an "optimistic deep" liberalization scenario, are rather limited for Brazil. Accordingly, poverty would remain largely unaffected by this trade reform, which does not appear to be biased in favor any of particularly poor groups. Yet, through a slight improvement in the urban income distribution the Doha scenario has some positive effect on poverty. In contrast, a full liberalization scenario that implies drastic domestic tariff cuts causes quite substantial welfare gains that are concentrated among some of the poorest groups of the country, in particular those in agriculture. Yet, relatively strong contractions in manufacturing sectors give reasons for concern.

---

19 This chapter forms part a major research program of The World Bank to assess the poverty impacts of a possible WTO agreement ("Doha" round). World market price changes caused by multilateral liberalization were calculated using a global CGE model and then passed to a number of single country cases. The results of all country case studies as well as a summary can be found in Hertel and Winters (2005). This book also contains a shorter summary version of chapter 3.

2. The poverty and distributional impact of "opening-up": Urban Colombia in the early 1990s

2.1. Introduction

Not only globalization critics are concerned when it comes to the poverty and distributional implications of trade liberalization in the developing world. It is widely acknowledged today that trade liberalization, at least in the short to medium run, may hurt some, possibly poor, economic actors. Its impact depends on a whole range of country-specific factors including the structure of protection in place and how this structure is affected by liberalization, the resulting price changes and price transmission, supply responses, and the functioning of labor markets.[20] In economies that are not dominated by household-based agricultural activities, the labor market acts as the major transmission channel of trade reforms on final welfare outcomes, although changes in relative goods prices can also have important welfare implications.

Trade reform triggers labor reallocations across sectors, and may cause (temporary) unemployment, or, when this is not an option, labor movements into informal employment. What regards changes in the distribution of wages[21], Stolper-Samuelson effects were long thought to work in favor of the poor in developing countries, as they should have led to real wage gains for (poor) unskilled labor. Unskilled labor was considered the factor used more intensively in the production of the goods in which developing countries supposedly had a comparative advantage. In the Latin American context, a number of reasons have been discussed why this story may well be too simple. First, with the entry of China into the world economy and in light of Latin America's abundant natural resources, the continent's comparative advantage by the late 1980s was not necessarily in the production of unskilled-labor-intensive products, as suggested by Wood (1997). A related second argument was raised by Feenstra and Hanson (1995) who show that Mexican exports are relatively skilled-labor-intensive, when judged by Mexican standards. Third, unskilled-labor-intensive industries, in particular light manufacturing, had been protected more heavily than more skill-intensive industries (Harrison 2005). These factors explain part of the increase in wage inequalities that have been observed in post-liberalization periods in Latin America. An additional, and possibly more important, source of increasing wage inequality is skill-biased technological change, which could be partly attributed to trade-liberalization.

Analyzing the impact of trade liberalization on employment, the distribution of wages, and relative prices can only be the first step in judging its poverty and distributional effects. In the second step, the implications on household welfare

---

20 In much more detail, the reasons why "it depends" are reviewed e.g. in Goldberg and Pavcnik (2004b), Harrison (2005) and Winters et al. (2004).

21 See Arbache et al. (2004) for a review of the effects of trade liberalization on the distribution of wages in developing countries.

need to be addressed, which is what this chapter intends to do for the case of the Colombian trade liberalization.

In the early 1990s, Colombia drastically reduced trade restrictions and implemented institutional as well as regulatory reforms. In addition to trade liberalization, the government undertook a series of other structural reforms ranging from capital account liberalization, foreign exchange deregulation, and financial markets reforms to a labor reform and major public sector restructuring. Economic reforms combined with the non-tradable boom brought substantial overall welfare gains to urban Colombians. Between 1988 and 1995, urban mean per capita income increased at an annual rate of approximately 3.2 percent and urban poverty declined significantly. Yet at the same time, inequality worsened considerably.[22]

Trade liberalization may have contributed to this increase in inequality and a series of papers by Goldberg and Pavcnik (2003, 2005) and Attanasio, Goldberg, and Pavcnik (2004) has examined the labor market impacts of the Colombian external liberalization. Attanasio et al. (2004) find trade liberalization to have affected the Colombian wage distribution through (1) increasing returns to college education, (2) wage decreases in sectors that initially exhibited lower wages, and (3) a shifts towards more informal employment. Yet, the effects are rather small and they conclude that trade liberalization has only played a minor role in explaining the observed worsening of the wage distribution in the early 1990s. In a more recent paper, Goldberg and Pavcnik (2004a) have tried to assess the implications of their findings on urban poverty. They compile poverty profiles in order to identify determinants of poverty that may be affected by trade liberalization and relate these determinants to their earlier findings on the labor market impacts. According to this "reduced form" approach, trade liberalization had, if at all, a negative impact on urban poverty, in particular through increasing informality.

In addition to these studies on the impact of trade, a number of studies (e.g. Ocampo et al. 2000, Vélez et al. 2005) have analyzed inequality and poverty changes in Colombia. Vélez et al. (2005) examine poverty and distributional dynamics during the reform period. Their "decomposition through microsimulation" approach allows them to identify and decompose the sources of observed distributional and poverty changes. They find the overall inequality increase between 1988 and 1995 to be the result of a number of counterbalancing forces. Widening rural-urban disparities as well as educational expansion in the presence of convex earnings with regard to education implied increasing inequality that was only slightly hampered by decreases in returns to education. Vélez et al. (2005) offer very interesting insights into the income distribution dynamics of Colombia. Yet, the study fails to link these observations to economic policy changes or external shocks.

---

22 See World Bank (2002), UNDP (1998), and Vélez et al. (2005) for detailed descriptions of poverty and distributional changes in this period.

In this chapter, we use a microsimulation model, which comprehensively models the household income generation process, to evaluate the impact of trade liberalization on poverty and the distribution of income in urban Colombia in the early 1990s.[23] The drivers of distributional change in the model are changes in employment, wages, and relative goods prices, which are linked to trade liberalization based on existing empirical studies. Since providing quantitative estimates of trade-induced labor market and price changes remains arbitrary to a certain extend, we complement these studies by discussions on the influence of other relevant factors and provide additional survey-based descriptive evidence. In particular, the approach taken in this chapter hence tries to close the gap between the evidence on the effects on wages and employment provided by Goldberg and Pavcnik (2003, 2005) and the final impact on poverty and the distribution of income. The chapter can be seen as an extension of the work by Vélez et al. (2005), as the microsimulation model is quite similar. Instead of simply decomposing distributional change, we attempt to link certain drivers of poverty and distributional change to trade liberalization. Our intention is not to construct one trade liberalization counterfactual, but rather to estimate the order of magnitude of the poverty and distributional implications of the respective labor market (and relative price) changes that we can relate to trade reform as well as the interactions between these changes. Furthermore, we assess the magnitude of these effects vis-à-vis poverty and distributional changes triggered by factors that cannot be related to trade liberalization. To this end, a number of hypothetical, although empirically motivated, scenarios with changes in earnings and employment as well as relative goods price changes are fed into the microsimulation, which then produces counterfactual income distributions.

The chapter is structured accordingly. We first review the Colombian trade reform of the early 1990s as well as accompanying structural reforms and shortly examine the macroeconomic context. We then describe the microsimulation model. The subsequent section discusses the poverty and distributional outcomes of the hypothetical scenarios. The final section summarizes the results and concludes with some tentative policy implications.

2.2.   Colombia in the early 1990s: "Apertura" and a non-tradable boom

In the early 1990s, the Colombian government under Cesar Gaviria implemented an ambitious structural reform program. Among the various reforms, of which most were put into effect under the 4 years of the Gaviria administration, the most relevant were the so-called "Apertura", which comprised a trade and capital account liberalization, and a major public sector reform. Further more moderate

---

23 We restrict our analysis to urban areas because of data shortcomings in rural areas, e.g. the lack of disaggregation of agricultural activities and of expenditure data, which make it impossible to trace the transmission channels of trade liberalization in the rural setting.

reform efforts include policies to increase domestic competition and a partial labor market reform.[24]

Colombia's trade reform was announced as a gradual and selective process that should have liberalized imports during a five-year period lasting until the end of 1994. Yet, macroeconomic imbalances forced the administration to change plans and the tariff schedule due in 1994 was already adopted in August 1991. The root cause of these difficulties was a real appreciation of the peso that undermined the government's intention to smooth adjustment to the trade reforms by a monetary policy aimed at a real depreciation. Efforts to devalue the peso were contrasted by increasing speculations of an appreciation, which were fuelled by the discovery of new oil fields. Facilitated by the opening of the capital account, large capital inflows and stagnating imports generated a balance of payment surplus that entailed international reserves accumulation. This situation created increasing difficulties of monetary management and, in September 1991, the government took the decision to drastically reduce tariffs almost overnight. Table 2.1 gives some indications of the magnitude of the "Apertura": in just a few months, nominal average tariffs were reduced from almost 40 percent to about 10 percent and the sectoral dispersion of the protection rates also went down, as shown by the reduction of the average effective rate from almost 70 percent to just 22 percent.

Table 2.1: Trade Liberalization in Colombia

Type of goods \ year	Nominal tariff rates %		Effective rates of protection %	
	1990	*1992*	*1990*	*1992*
Consumption goods	53	17	109	37
Intermediate inputs	36	10	61	18
Capital goods	34	10	48	15
Total	39	12	67	22

Source: Bussolo and Lay (2005).

Quantitative restrictions were almost completely eliminated as well. Before Gaviria took office, 50 percent of all imports were subject to import licensing; only one year later less than 3 percent of imports were still under such a scheme. The reduction of import tariffs and quantitative restrictions was complemented with other measures including regulatory changes, as anti-dumping and other unfair competition, institutional reform, including the creation of a new independent Ministry of Foreign Trade, and, finally, the stipulation of international trade treaties, as the free trade agreement (FTA) with Venezuela in 1991, the contemporary reviving of the Andean Pact, another FTA with Chile in 1993, and the Group of 3 treaty with Mexico and Venezuela in 1994.

To evaluate the impact of the trade reform, not only the scale and scope of the trade reform itself have to be taken into account, but also additional structural reforms as well as the macroeconomic context. The late 80's and the beginning of

---

24 See Ocampo (1999) for a detailed description of the reforms.

the 90's witnessed a series of other important structural reforms. Many of these affected the role of the public sector and regulations, such as central bank independence, decentralization, social security and tax reforms, housing policy changes, as well as changes in financial sector and port regulations. In addition, external liberalization was not restricted to the current account. Foreign exchange controls were reduced and capital transactions were liberalized although certain restrictions on capital inflows were maintained. Furthermore, public expenditure increased substantially in the early 1990s from approx. 30 percent of GDP in 1988 to 34 percent in 1995. This expansion was largely financed by higher public revenues following the mentioned tax reforms. Fluctuations in international prices for coffee and oil, which in 1991 accounted for approximately 40 percent of Colombian exports, also affected the Colombian economy.[25] Yet, Colombian economic performance in the early 1990s, in particular in urban areas, was dominated by a consumption boom with aggregate consumption growing by almost 10 percent annually between 1992 and 1995. Consumption growth was fuelled by capital inflows as well as increased public spending and translated into strong growth of the non-tradable economy. In sum, the Colombian economy in the early 1990s was characterized by an appreciated exchange rate and a vibrant non-tradable economy.

Although the introduction of the "Apertura" policy package was triggered by macroeconomic imbalances, its main objective was to stimulate growth and to improve the distribution of income. Growth effects were expected from (1) the reallocation of resources towards more productive uses according to price signals from international markets, (2) increased competition, and (3) technology transfer that would be enhanced by increased private capital inflows. Inequality would have decreased if unskilled labor had benefited from increased specialization towards labor intensive industries. Together, growth and lower inequality would have reduced poverty.

In the macroeconomic context described above, labor reallocation processes after trade liberalization were dominated by employment destruction in formerly protected sectors and employment creation in non-tradable sectors, particularly in informal activities. The driving forces were increased international competition as well as the real appreciation. As protection patterns were biased towards labor intensive sectors, unskilled labor was affected more by this decline in tradable sector employment also putting pressure on unskilled wages. This distributionally unfavorable effect was reinforced by skill-biased technological change that is likely to be related to trade liberalization and increasing capital inflows. All in all, the effects of trade liberalization, which we will analyze in much more detail below, did hence not correspond to the expectations.

---

25 Between 1991 and 1993, hence during the period of liberalization, coffee prices (Arabica prices paid to Colombian growers) declined by approx. 25 percent. Due to a frost in Brazil prices more than doubled between January and December 1994.

2.3.   Capturing the transmission channels: Methodology

This section describes the microsimulation model that we use to simulate and decompose the poverty and distributional impact of trade liberalization. The general principle of the model is that, based on a household income generation model, individual labor earnings adjust to produce changes in the following aggregates: (1) changes in average wages in different wage labor market segments, (2) changes in profits from self-employment, (3) changes in employment shares in different labor market segments, i.e. the shares of wage-earners, self-employed, and inactive individuals per segment. Furthermore, resulting household incomes are deflated taking into account (4) changes in food vs. non-food prices. Later, we will construct counterfactual scenarios of changes in these aggregate variables that we attempt to link to trade liberalization.

In the microsimulation, we hence model the household income generation process.[26] This implies that individuals make occupational choices and earn wages or profits accordingly. These labor market incomes plus exogenous other incomes, such as transfers and imputed housing rents, comprise household income. The major advantage of using microsimulation techniques is that the poverty and distributional impact of policies, as in reality, will depend on the characteristics of the households or even individuals. In other words, the microsimulation takes into account both individual and household heterogeneity. Individual heterogeneity refers to personal characteristics, which influence occupational choices and income generated on the labor market. Occupational choices are subject to a number of factors, which include gender, marital status, or age of children. Important determinants of labor income are education and experience. Household heterogeneity is reflected, for example, in different sources of income and demographic composition. Furthermore, the microsimulation captures some household heterogeneity in terms of expenditure structure.

The components of the income generation model are an occupational choice and an earnings model. In the choice model, individual agents can choose between inactivity, wage-employment, and self-employment.[27] The occupational choice model is assumed to be slightly different for household heads, spouses, and other family members. Once occupational choices are made, earnings are generated accordingly either in the form of wages or as profits for the self-employed. Being self-employed means being part of what might be called a "household-enterprise", in which all self-employed members of a household pool their incomes. The wage-employment market is segmented: the wage setting mechanisms are assumed to

---

26   The following section borrows from Robilliard et al. (2002). A more detailed discussion of a similar labor market specification can be found in Alatas and Bourguignon (2005).

27   Throughout the chapter, we will use self-employment and informal sector employment interchangeably; well aware that there are many dimensions of informality.

differ for skilled and unskilled labor as well as for females and males, which implies that there are four wage labor market segments.

The following set of equations describes the model. Household m has k_m members, which are indexed by i.

$$\log w_{mi} = a_{g(mi)} + x_{mi}\beta_{g(mi)} + e_{mi} \tag{1}$$

$$\log \pi_m = b_m + z_m \delta_m + \lambda_m N_m + \varepsilon_m \tag{2}$$

$$Y_m = \frac{1}{P_m}\left(\sum_{i=1}^{k_m} w_{mi} IW_{mi} + \pi_m Ind(N_m > 0) + y_{0m}\right) \tag{3}$$

$$P_m = s_{d(m)} p_f + \left(1 - s_{d(m)}\right) p_{nf} \tag{4}$$

$$IW_{mi} = Ind\left[c_{h(mi)}^w + z_{mi}\alpha_{h(mi)}^w + u_{mi}^w > Sup\left(0, c_{h(mi)}^s + z_{mi}\alpha_{h(mi)}^s + u_{mi}^s\right)\right] \tag{5}$$

$$N_m = \sum_{i=1}^{k_m} Ind\left[c_{h(mi)}^s + z_{mi}\alpha_{h(mi)}^s + u_{mi}^s > Sup\left(0, c_{h(mi)}^w + z_{mi}\alpha_{h(mi)}^w + u_{mi}^w\right)\right] \tag{6}$$

The first equation is a Mincerian wage equation, where the log wage of member i of household m depends on his/her personal characteristics. The explanatory variables include schooling years, experience, the squared terms of these two variables, and a set of regional dummies. This wage equation is estimated for each of the four labor market segments. The index function *g(mi)* assigns individual i in household m to a specific labor market segment. The residual term e_{mi} describes unobserved earnings determinants.

The second equation represents the profit function of household m. Profits are earned if at least one member of the household is self-employed. The profit function is of a Mincer type and includes as explanatory variables the schooling of the household head, her/his experience plus the squared terms the former two variables, and regional dummies. Of course, profits also depend on the number of self-employed in household m, N_m. The residual ε_m captures unobserved effects.

Household income is defined by the third equation. It consists of the wages and profits earned by the household members and an exogenous income y_{0m}. This exogenous income corresponds to "other income" in the survey and may include government transfers, transfers from abroad, capital income, etc.. IW_{mi} is a dummy variable that equals 1 if member i of the household is wage-employed and 0 otherwise. Likewise, profits will only be earned if at least one family member is self-employed ($N_m>0$). Household income is deflated by a household specific price index, which is defined by equation (4). The parameter s denotes the expenditure shares for food- and non-food. These shares are calculated by household income quintiles. Note that the prices p_f for food and p_{nf} will be 1 initially. The index function $d(m)$ indicates to which of the five income brackets household m belongs and which food expenditure share is assigned to the household.

The fifth equation explains the aforementioned dummy IW_{mi}. The individual will be wage-employed if the utility associated with wage-employment is higher than the utility of being self-employed or inactive. The utility of being inactive is arbitrarily set to zero, whereas the utilities of the employment options depend on a set of personal and household characteristics, z_{mi}. These characteristics include gender, marital status, education, experience, other income, the educational attainments of other household members, and the number of children. Unobserved determinants of occupational choices are represented by the residuals.

Equation (6) gives the number of self-employed. Similar to the choice in equation (5), the individual i of household m will prefer self-employment if the associated utility is higher than the utility of inactivity or wage-employment. The self-employed household members form the "household enterprise" with N_m working members. Thus, the last two equations represent the occupational choices of the household members. The occupational choice model is estimated separately for household heads, spouses, and other household members in urban and rural areas. The index function $h(mi)$ assigns the individual to the corresponding group.

The model just described gives the household income as a non-linear function of individual and household characteristics, unobserved characteristics, and the household budget shares. This function depends on three sets of parameters, which are estimated based on the 1988 survey. These parameters include (1) the parameters of the wage equation for each labor market segment, (2) the parameters of the profit function for "household enterprises", (3) the parameters in the utility associated with different occupational choices for heads, spouses, and other family members.

The income generation model requires some comments on the assumptions behind its formulation. First of all, despite the availability of data on working time we decided to model the occupational choice as a discrete choice.[28] Secondly, our model assumes that the Colombian labor market is segmented along different lines. One line of segmentation separates wage-employment from self-employment. In a perfectly competitive labor market, the returns to labor would be equal for these two types of employment. Yet, segmentation may be justified because income from self-employment is likely to contain a rent from non-labor assets used, and its clearing mechanism may differ from that of wage employment. Information on non-labor assets is not available for Colombia, hence distinct equations need to be estimated even if the labor markets were competitive. In addition, even in those cases where information on non-labor assets is available, a segmented labor market can be justified by the fact that wage-employment may be rationed and self-employment thus "absorbs" those who do not get a job in the preferred wage work. Wage work could be preferred for generating a more steady

---

28 However, estimating wage equations based on hourly wages did not make a major
    difference in the coefficients.

income stream or for fringe benefits related to this type of employment. Conversely, self-employment might exhibit important externalities, for example for households, in which children have to be taken care of. Self-employment of the household head may also create employment opportunities for other family members. Additional segmentation is assumed within the wage labor market. The segmentation hypothesis along the lines of skills and gender is strongly supported by the regression results.

In a first step, the occupational choice model and the wage and profits equations are estimated in order to obtain an initial set of coefficients (a_G, β_G, b_F, δ_F, $c_H{}^w$, $\alpha_H{}^w$, $c_H{}^s$, $\alpha_H{}^s$) and unobserved characteristics (e_{mi}, ε_m, $u^w{}_{mi}$, $u^s{}_{mi}$).[29] The income generation model is estimated using data from the Colombian household survey from 1988.[30] The estimated benchmark coefficients are then employed and changed in the micro-simulation. Unobserved characteristics say for the wage equation can of course only be obtained for those who are actually wage-employed. For self-employed or inactive individuals the unobserved characteristics in the wage-equations are randomly drawn from normal distributions with the respective estimated error variances. In the same way, we generate unobserved characteristics for the profit function for households without a household enterprise. As we estimate wage and profit functions using ordinary least squares (or 2 SLS), these unobserved characteristics are assumed to be normally distributed as well, again with the estimated error variances. Additionally, unobserved characteristics (or utility) need to be generated for the occupational choice model. In latent utility models, these residuals cannot be observed and are hence generated from the distribution underlying the respective model. The multinomial choice model assumes that errors follow the Gumbel (or type I extreme value) distribution.[31] Residuals have to be drawn consistent with the observed occupational choice, i.e. the utility an observed wage earner relates to

29 The occupational choice model was estimated using a multinomial logit. The wage equations were estimated by Ordinary Least Squares. Correcting for selection bias in these equations did not lead to major changes in the results and was hence dropped. In the estimation of the profit functions, the number of self-employed was instrumented. The estimation results for the wage and profit equations as well as for the occupational choice models are reported in App. Table 2.2 and App. Table 2.3. For a more detailed discussion of the estimation methods see Bourguignon and Ferreira (2005).

30 The household survey used for estimation of the micro-simulation parameters is the Colombian Encuesta Nacional de Hogares from 1988 (EH61). After the removal of outliers, removal of individuals with top-coded earnings, and observations with missing data the survey covers 29 729 individuals living in 12 092 households in urban areas. The household weights are adjusted for the removed observations. The expenditure shares are calculated from an income and expenditure survey and matched with the EH61 based on household groups, classified according to income quintiles. For the problems of these datasets see Núñez and Jiménez (1997).

31 The variance of this distribution is $\pi^2/6$. Train (2003) contains a detailed (and accessible) discussion about the distributional assumption of logit models.

wage-employment has to be higher than the utility associated with inactivity or self-employment. Statistically, this implies to draw these residuals conditional on the observed choice. We apply a method proposed by Bourguignon, Fournier and Gurgand (1998), who show how to obtain these conditional draws from a Gumbel distribution.[32]

In the simulation, changes in aggregate variables are used as target values. Individual earnings and occupational choices change to reach these targets on the aggregate level. The required individual changes are obtained by varying coefficients in the occupational choice and the earnings models. In other words, coefficients are adjusted and occupational choices and earnings change accordingly, until the results of the micro-simulation are consistent, at an aggregate level, with the given aggregates. Formally, the following constraints describe the consistency requirements. Let the right hand side variables describe the initial aggregate values, where E_G corresponds to the number of wage-employed, S_G, the number of self-employed, w_G, the sum of wages paid in segment G, π_F, the sum of profits paid in activity F. "G" stands for the eight labor market segments, i.e. urban male skilled and unskilled, urban female skilled and unskilled, rural male skilled and unskilled, rural female skilled and unskilled labor. Note that $\wedge$ indicates that the coefficients, residuals, and indicator function values result from the estimation described above.

$$\sum_m \sum_{i,g(mi)=G} \hat{IW}_{mi} =$$

$$\sum_m \sum_{i,g(mi)=G} Ind\left[\hat{c}^w_{h(mi)} + z_{mi}\hat{\alpha}^w_{h(mi)} + \hat{u}^w_{mi} > Sup\left(0, \hat{c}^s_{h(mi)} + z_{mi}\hat{\alpha}^s_{h(mi)} + \hat{u}^s_{mi}\right)\right] = E_G$$

$$(7)$$

$$\sum_m \sum_{i,g(mi)=G} Ind\left[\hat{c}^s_{h(mi)} + z_{mi}\hat{\alpha}^s_{h(mi)} + \hat{u}^s_{mi} > Sup\left(0, \hat{c}^w_{h(mi)} + z_{mi}\hat{\alpha}^w_{h(mi)} + \hat{u}^w_{mi}\right)\right] = S_G$$

$$(8)$$

$$\sum_m \sum_{i,g(mi)=G} exp\left(\hat{a}_G + x_{mi}\hat{\beta}_G + \hat{e}_{mi}\right)\hat{IW}_{mi} = w_G \qquad (9)$$

$$\sum_m exp\left(\hat{b}^*_G + z_m\hat{\partial}_G + \hat{\varepsilon}_m\right)Ind\left(N_m > 0\right) = \pi^* \qquad (10)$$

---

32 Another ad-hoc approach would use a random number generator for the Gumbel distribution (u=-log(-log(x)) where x is a random draw from a uniform distribution), and repeatedly draw residuals until the observed choices correspond to the simulated ones.

The liberalization shock now produces changes in these aggregates and in the price vector. The result is a new vector of these variables, which will be identified by an asterisk (E^*_G, S^*_G, w^*_G, π^*). For the above constraints to hold, an appropriate vector of coefficients and prices (a_G, β_G, b, δ, c_H^w, α_H^w, c_H^s, α_H) is needed. For these coefficients, many solutions exist and additional constraints have to be introduced. As in Robilliard et al. (2002) our choice is to vary the constants (a_G, b, c^w_H, c^s_H) and leave the other coefficients unchanged. We hence assume that the changes in occupational choices and earnings are dependent on personal and household characteristics only to a limited degree. Changing the intercept in one of the wage equations implies that all individuals of the respective segment experience the same increase in log earnings. This increase does not depend on individual characteristics. The same holds for the profit function. Consistency of the microsimulation and the new aggregates hence requires the solution of the following system of equations. This is the way the microsimulation is "forced" to reproduce given changes in aggregate variables.

$$\sum_{m}\sum_{i,g(mi)=G}\hat{IW}_{mi} =$$
$$\sum_{m}\sum_{i,g(mi)=G} Ind\left[c^{*w}_{h(mi)} + z_{mi}\hat{\alpha}^w_{h(mi)} + \hat{u}^w_{mi} > Sup\left(0, c^{*s}_{h(mi)} + z_{mi}\hat{\alpha}^s_{h(mi)} + \hat{u}^s_{mi}\right)\right] = E^*_G$$

(11)

$$\sum_{m}\sum_{i,g(mi)=G} Ind\left[c^{*s}_{h(mi)} + z_{mi}\hat{\alpha}^s_{h(mi)} + \hat{u}^s_{mi} > Sup\left(0, c^{*w}_{h(mi)} + z_{mi}\hat{\alpha}^w_{h(mi)} + \hat{u}^w_{mi}\right)\right] = S^*_G$$

(12)

$$\sum_{m}\sum_{i,g(mi)=G} exp\left(a^*_G + x_{mi}\hat{\beta}_G + \hat{e}_{mi}\right)\hat{IW}_{mi} = w^*_G$$

(13)

$$\sum_{m} exp\left(b^*_G + z_m\hat{\partial}_G + \hat{\varepsilon}_m\right)Ind\left(N_m > 0\right) = \pi^*$$

(14)

Equations (11) and (12) require the number of self-employed and wage-employed to be consistent with the target values for each of the four segments (G). This also holds for the wage equation for each of the segments and the profit function, as indicated by equations (13) and (14). Hence, the above system contains 13 restrictions. The system has four unknown constants in the wage equations, one in the profit function, and 8 in the occupational choice model.[33]

Thus we have 13 unknown constants and 13 equations. We obtain the solution by applying standard Gauss-Newton techniques.

Solving the above system gives us a new set of constants (a^{*}_{G}, b^{*}, c^{*w}_{H}, c^{*s}_{H}), which is then used to compute occupational choices, wages, and profits. Additionally, changes in relative prices of food and non-food items are taken into account by deflating the resulting household incomes by household group specific price indices.

Before we turn to the simulations we shortly would like to point to some of the shortcomings of the model. First, we just differentiate between formal and informal employment defined by being wage- or self-employed. Yet, income differences also exist e.g. between manufacturing and personal service sectors and these sectoral wage differences are ignored. In addition, self-employment activities are very heterogeneous, which is only rudimentarily reflected in the model. An interesting extension of the income generation model would hence be to differentiate between subsistence-oriented and other self-employment activities. A more general second set of drawbacks of the microsimulation is its reliance on one cross-section and the assumption of constant behavioral parameters. Choosing the constants in the occupational choice and earnings equations to vary is an additional rather restrictive assumption. It implies that the within-group wage distribution only changes through entry and exit of individuals with certain characteristics and not, for example, through changes in returns to education. This may not be relevant for unskilled labor, but certainly for skilled labor in the considered period. A related third shortcoming regards the use of an occupational choice model, which is estimated comparing occupational "states", to simulate occupational transition. For example, the simulation makes those women move into employment first, who are relatively unlikely to be inactive; these are ceteris paribus more educated women. Whether it is the more educated who, in reality, move into employment may depend a lot on how the shock impacts on labor demand. A final point should be made on the rudimentary nature of the model with regard to the expenditure side. Expenditure shares, which are only defined by income quintile, are fixed, i.e. substitution is not allowed for. Furthermore, we only consider two price indices based on baskets of food and non-food items. Household heterogeneity in terms of consumption patterns is hence quite limited.

2.4.   The poverty and distributional impact of "Apertura"

To set the stage for the following analysis, we examine the composition of income of urban households by the sources that we distinguish in our analysis, i.e. wage income from unskilled/skilled male/female labor as well as "informal" profits from self-employment and exogenous other income. Figure 2.1 shows the composition of household income by per capita income vintiles. As expected, informal profits constitute the main share of income for the poorer parts of the population. The poorest 5 percent of households derive almost half of their income from self-employment. Unskilled male wage-employment accounts for most of the income earned by poorer households, whereas male as well as female skilled wage income is an important income source only for the richest 20 percent of the population. Unskilled female wage income is most important for the urban middle class.

Figure 2.1: Composition of income by source by income vintile

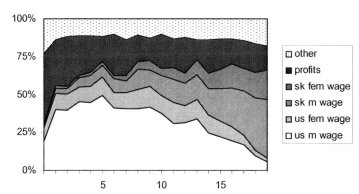

Source: Author's calculations.

The historical scenario: To put the effects of trade liberalization into perspective, we construct a historical labor market scenario by comparing the 1988 and the 1995 survey. In terms of employment composition, the most remarkable development in the early 1990s is the sharp increase of self-employment across all labor market segments, which for both male unskilled and skilled workers is at the expense of wage-employment (Table 2.2). Female labor market participation increases considerably, especially in self-employment activities.[34]

Table 2.2: Labor force composition in 1988 and 1995

	1988 initial shares			1988-95 point change in shares		
	Inactive	*Wage-work*	*Self-empl.*	*Inactive*	*Wage-work*	*Self-empl.*
Unskilled male	6.5	6.5	32.3	-0.3	-5.8	6.1
Skilled male	7.6	7.6	19.5	0.1	-3.0	2.9
Unskilled female	64.3	64.3	13.9	-6.8	2.1	4.7
Skilled female	48.6	48.6	9.3	-2.4	-0.5	2.9
Total urban	32.5	32.5	17.3	-4.0	0.2	3.8

Source: Author's calculations.

Note: The right panel of the table displays the percentage point change with regard to the initial occupational category shares.

---

34 Our results are consistent with former studies, although comparability is limited due to the different segmentation choices. For an overview of labor market indicators for 1988 and 1995 see Vélez et al. (2005). Ocampo et al. (2000) additionally consider the sectoral composition of employment.

Table 2.3: Real wages and self-employment income, 1988 and 1988-95 evolution

	Initial	1988-95 change
Wage		
Unskilled male	40 659	2.4
Skilled male	85 331	6.5
Unskilled female	30 316	-4.8
Skilled female	57 272	6.8
Self-empl. income	44 071	13.0

Source: Author's calculations.

Note: the second column shows percent changes.

Table 2.3 reports (cumulative) income changes by labor market segments between 1988 and 1995. For both males and females the wage gap between unskilled and skilled labor increases considerably. This increase is more pronounced for females, as unskilled female wages even decline, which may also be caused by unskilled female entrants in the lower parts of the wage distribution. Whereas unskilled male wages grow only slightly in the period under consideration, informal profits increase substantially. These historical labor market aggregate changes should be interpreted with some caution, as they are just based on two surveys.

We now pass these historical changes in employment and earnings to the microsimulation model to test whether the model is adequate to reproduce distributional and poverty change. Such an exercise will hence illustrate whether there are distributional changes the methodology cannot trace. Overall, this validation exercise suggests that the admittedly simple income generation model does reasonably well in capturing the forces of distributional change that are considered key transmission channels of trade liberalization.

In Figure 2.2, we plot growth incidence curves of historical (based on the 1988 and the 1995 household survey) and of simulated per capita income changes. Overall, the microsimulation gives lower growth in per capita incomes than could be observed historically (see also Table 2.4). This is not too surprising, since human and physical capital accumulation is partly ignored in the model. For example, the simulation does not reflect the considerable educational expansion between 1988 and 1995 that is also reflected in a marked increase in the share of skilled labor (App. Table 2.1). The distributional effect of this expansion is negative, since earnings are highly convex in years of schooling. This convexity implies that (wage) inequality increases if educational endowments of every individual increase by a constant greater than 1. Actually, the distribution of years of schooling became more equal between 1988 and 1995, which could not offset

Figure 2.2:   Growth incidence curves, real data vs. historical simulation 1988-95
(5ᵗʰ to 95ᵗʰ percentile)³⁵

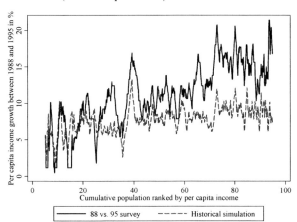

Source: Author's calculations.

the unequalizing effect of higher mean education.[36] This also explains why the gap between the historical and simulated growth incidence curves widens with rising income. Another phenomenon that the simulation does not capture is rural-urban migration, which is likely to increase the number of rather young and relatively uneducated individuals in urban areas. Despite these shortcomings, the microsimulation quite well reflects the structure of distributional change, in particular the "steps" in the historical growth incidence curve around the 40ᵗʰ and the 75ᵗʰ percentile. Furthermore, it reproduces oscillating income changes in the lower parts of the distribution and even traces some of the spikes of the historical

---

35 For expositional purposes, we only plot the curves from the 5th to the 95th percentile. The entire curves can be found in App. Figure 2.1. For both the lowest and highest percentiles there are larger deviations between the simulation and real data. For the lowest percentile, the historical data shows a substantial decrease between 1988 and 1995. In addition, the microsimulation cannot capture the very large per capita increases in the highest percentiles. We can only speculate on the extremely high negative (for the poor) and positive (for the rich) growth rates found in the historical data. While conflict-induced migration of poor migrants into the cities may well be a reason for negative growth at the bottom of the distribution, the high growth rates for the rich may arise from data deficiencies. For 1995 we have to drop 80 observations due to top-coding, while for 1988 the number amounts to 122, with roughly the same sample size. Despite our efforts to adjust the household weights for dropped observations, this might explain part of the observed increase. Although this merits further investigation it is not crucial to the question examined here.

36 For details see Vélez et al. (2005) and the summary chapter in Bourguignon, Ferreira, and Lustig (2005a).

growth incidence curve. Yet, the differences between the "real" and the simulated historical scenario are also reflected in the aggregate indicators reported in Table 2.4 . The relatively pronounced differences in poverty reduction are mainly due to the failure of the microsimulation to capture the spike in the "real" growth incidence curve around the 30th percentile. Whereas the Gini-Index remains constant in the microsimulation, the survey data shows a considerable increase. In the microsimulation, the positive distributional impact of increasing informal profits and increasing female labor market participation hence compensate the negative effects of a rising wage-gap and increasing informality. In reality, educational expansion and very high growth rates of incomes in the highest ten percentiles, which the microsimulation fails to capture (or which may partly be due to data deficiencies), dominate distributional outcomes.

Table 2.4:   *Poverty and distributional simulation results, real data vs. historical simulation 1988-95*

| | Per capita income | % point change in index | | | | |
| | | Poverty | | | Inequality | |
		P0	P1	P2	Gini	Theil
Initial	21899.6	60.4	26.5	14.9	39.9	46.7
1995	18.0	-6.8	-4.2	-2.7	3.2	
Hist sim	7.3	-3.8	-2.3	-1.4	0.0	-0.1

Source: Author's calculation.

While the above historical scenario reflects all policy changes and shocks, the following discussion intends to evaluate employment and earnings changes attributable to trade liberalization. We review existing evidence that we complement by own descriptive survey-based evidence. First, we consider liberalization-induced changes in the employment structure, i.e. employment creation or destruction and associated increases/decreases in unemployment or employment shifts between formal and informal activities. We then discuss earnings changes.

The impact of trade liberalization varied considerably across sectors. According to Ocampo (1999), light manufacturing, such as apparel and leather, was mainly hurt through the real appreciation, whereas heavy manufacturing faced strong import competition. This competitive effect was reinforced again by the appreciation. The contraction in the manufacturing sectors also translated into a reduction of wage-employment and hence to informalization.[37] In light manufacturing, informal female employment shrank massively, which is very likely to reflect job losses for self-employed women who are sub-contracted for work at home in the leather and apparel sector. The data however suggests that these job losses have not been associated with an increase in unemployment, in line with findings by Attanasio et al. (2004). The losses of wage-employment in

---

37   See the changes in the sectoral composition of employment by labor market segment reported in App. Table 2.4.

manufacturing were hence compensated either by employment creation in other sectors, mainly in services, and increased informal employment. As the share of informal employment increases in the sectors that are affected by trade liberalization, the informal sector hence partly functions as a within-industry labor sink, a view supported empirically by Goldberg and Pavcnik (2003). There is no evidence of employment creation in export-oriented sectors.

Whereas urban sectoral employment changes can be linked to trade reform reasonably well, determining the order of magnitude of earnings changes in different labor market segments that are due to the reform is more challenging. Goldberg and Pavcnik (2005) and Attanasio et al. (2004) find trade reforms to be associated with an increase in wage inequality. Among other things, this increase is caused by decreasing industry wage premia in unskilled-labor intensive sectors caused by relatively large tariff cuts in those sectors. Unfortunately, Attanasio et al. (2004) do not report the relative importance of these premia in wages, but some own exploratory regressions (not reported) suggest that they are of minor quantitative importance. Hence, even if trade policy changes have a significant (unequalizing) effect on industry wage premia, the effect on the wage distribution may be rather small. The final impact on the distribution of per capita incomes is then likely to be even negligible. On the contrary, a major force behind increasing inequality is the increasing wage-gap between unskilled and skilled labor, whose negative distributional impact is reinforced by the unequal expansion of educational endowments. According to Attanasio et al. (2004), the increasing skill premium is primarily driven by skill-biased technological change. In how far the skill bias can be ascribed to trade reform is less clear, but there is evidence that the sectors with the largest reductions in tariffs were those with the sharpest increase in the share of skilled labor.[38] Another source of the increasing wage-gap that can be more closely related to trade reform is the relative shift in labor demand due to sectoral reallocations. Contracting manufacturing sectors use unskilled labor more intensively, as illustrated in App. Table 2.6.

In order to judge the impact of trade reform on relative wages, it is also instructive to consider other factors that have affected the supply and demand for unskilled and skilled labor, respectively. One important factor certainly was the boom in non-tradables. The sectors that most benefited from this boom were construction, as well as financial, government, and telecommunication services (Ocampo 1999). This suggests that the associated pattern of labor demand growth may have been slightly biased towards skilled wage labor. Yet, the strong increase in informal profits due to the boom should have had an indirect positive effect on unskilled wages. Overall, the non-tradables boom is hence likely to have affected the wage distribution rather positively. Furthermore, educational expansion, in contrast to its negative "endowment effect", should have an equalizing effect on relative wages through increasing the supply of skilled labor. In sum, other factors

---

38 Compared to most other sectors, we also find a relatively strong increase in the share of skilled labor in manufacturing sectors. App. Table 2.6.

beyond trade liberalization and technological change thus tend to have an equalizing effect on the wage-distribution.

Finally, we shortly provide evidence on relative goods price changes in the period under consideration. Between 1988 and 1995, nominal food (non-food) prices increased by a factor of 4.4 (5.1).[39] When the relative price between food and non-food items is assumed to be 1 in the base period, this roughly gives a relative price decrease of 15 points. While prices for non-tradable food crops increased in the early 1990s, prices for importables decreased substantially and imports of cereals, cereal products, soy beans, and fruits surged (Jaramillo 2001). Trade liberalization is hence very likely to explain most of the relative price decrease of foodstuff.

Starting from the above discussion, we now simulate "opening-up" counterfactual income distributions based on five different labor market and relative price change scenarios. More specifically, we first illustrate the poverty and distributional impact of trade-induced informalization, and examine the role of increasing informal profits in cushioning possible adverse effects of this process. We then attempt to quantify the impact of the increasing skilled-unskilled wage-gap. Finally, we assess the role of relative price changes.

The simulated scenarios are summarized in Table 2.5 and the corresponding changes in poverty and distributional indicators are reported in Table 2.6. In all the simulations, we chose to approximate the trade-induced losses in wage-employment by the losses in manufacturing wage-employment (reported in App. Table 2.4). As there is no indication of significant employment creation due to trade liberalization, labor market participation does not change in the simulations. As regards the effect of trade liberalization on relative wages, the above discussion demonstrates the difficulties of constructing a trade counterfactual. Yet, the main unequalizing forces at work, i.e. sectoral growth patterns and technological change, can at least partly be attributed to trade liberalization. This is why we approximate trade-induced changes in wage inequality by historical changes.[40] The income growth rates are chosen such that per capita growth would be equal across the simulations if there were no shifts between formal and informal employment. In other words, would we increase only wage labor incomes and informal profits by the rates given in Table 2.5, we would have the same per capita growth in Sim II to Sim IV. The benchmark growth rate was computed from Sim IV.

---

39 Information on changes in consumer prices by commodity groups from the Banco de la República (www.banrep.org) and on index-weights from the Departamento Administrativo Nacional de Estadística (DANE) at www.dane.gov.co.

40 Whether general technological change, which would have taken place with or without external liberalization, was the major factor is of course an open question. Yet, we find this unlikely in the time horizon under consideration. More precisely, we could say that the historical worsening of the wage distribution represent a lower bound of a "trade-cum-technological-change" scenario.

Table 2.5: Overview of simulation scenarios

		Usk m	Sk m	Usk f	Sk f	Profits	Rel. food price
% point change in wage-employment share (the same across all sims)		-2.9	-1.2	-3.3	0.0		
% change in wages/profits	Sim I	0.0	0.0	0.0	0.0	0.0	1.00
	Sim II	6.0	6.0	6.0	6.0	6.0	1.00
	Sim III	4.0	4.0	4.0	4.0	13.0	1.00
	Sim IV	2.4	6.5	-4.8	6.8	13.0	1.00
	Sim V	2.4	6.5	-4.8	6.8	13.0	0.86

Source: Author's calculations.

Table 2.6: Poverty and distributional simulation results

	Per capita income	% point change in index				
		Poverty			Inequality	
		P0	P1	P2	Gini	Theil
Initial	21899.6	60.4	26.5	14.9	39.9	46.7
Historical sim	7.3	-3.8	-2.3	-1.4	0.0	-0.1
Sim I	-0.3	0.1	0.4	0.3	0.3	0.3
Sim II	4.8	-2.3	-1.3	-0.8	0.2	0.2
Sim III	4.9	-2.4	-1.4	-0.9	0.1	0.1
Sim IV	5.3	-2.1	-1.2	-0.8	0.5	0.8
Sim V	4.5	-2.2	-1.4	-1.0	0.0	0.0

Source: Author's calculations.

In Sim I, we assess the impact of increasing informality by simulating an increase in self-employment while keeping average income from all sources constant. The simulated increase implies a per capita income decrease, as individuals move into employment with lower average earnings. The headcount index almost remains constant, but the poverty gap indicator increases by 0.4 percentage points. The increase in self-employment hence slightly causes the intensity of poverty to rise. The income losses in lower income groups also explain why inequality increases somewhat. By how much earnings decline due to becoming informal depends on individual characteristics. Yet, not only do the returns to individual characteristics change when an individual moves into informality. The move also involves an absolute income loss, which in relative terms becomes more important the poorer the household is. In addition, poorer individuals are more likely to move into informality. These three factors explain the worrisome decrease of per capita incomes in the lowest parts of the income distribution in this simulation.

While in Sim II all income sources grow by the same rate, Sim III takes into account the differential growth rates between wage and self-employment income (abstracting from the rising unskilled-skilled wage gap). Aggregate indicators remain virtually unchanged between the two simulations. Comparing the resulting growth incidence curves in App. Figure 2.2 gives a more nuanced picture. The comparison shows that the income losses in the lower parts of the distribution are somewhat lower but persist, i.e. for households with very low incomes the income losses due to higher self-employment cannot be compensated by higher self-employment income. Overall however, the distribution of income growth between self-employment and wage-employment matters surprisingly little in terms of poverty and distributional outcome.

In Sim IV, wages grow at the observed historical rates instead of equal rates, as in Sim III. Per capita income growth is 0.4 points higher in this simulation, as higher incomes grow at higher rates. At the same time, poverty reduction is lower and inequality increases quite considerably. Among the poor, income for households close to the poverty line declines most, as implied by the less pronounced differences in P1 and P2. These households are hit most by the dramatic decline in female unskilled wages. Overall, the isolated poverty impact of the increasing wage inequality does not seem to be too pronounced. Yet, the increase of inequality is quite substantial. This appears even more worrisome, as the simulation does neither account for educational expansion nor for increasing wage-inequality among skilled labor that is behind the extreme increase of per capita incomes in the highest vintile of the income distribution.

Interesting insights can also be gained from comparing Sim IV and the historical simulation. These two simulations only differ in occupational choice changes. We know from the above discussion that an increase in informality does not have major distributional implications (except for the lower parts of the distribution). Increasing female labor market participation hence explains most of the striking differences in outcomes between these two simulations.[41] Per capita income is significantly higher and inequality remains constant in the historical simulation. Increased female labor market participation, which cannot be linked to trade liberalization, hence plays an extremely important role in cushioning the negative distributional implications of increasing wage-inequality.

Sim V adds changes in relative goods prices to Sim IV. The decrease of food vis-à-vis non-food prices eliminates the negative distributional impact of higher informality and increasing wage inequality. The comparison of the growth incidence curves of Sim IV and Sim V (App. Table 2.6) shows that the implied real income loss for households in the highest two deciles amounts to approx. 2 percentage points in growth, while the poorest 40 percent gain around 1 percentage point. The effects on aggregate poverty indicators are rather small.

---

41   Veléz et al. (2005) also find female labor market entry among poor households to be a strongly equalizing force on per capita incomes.

2.5. Conclusions

The quantitative assessment of the poverty and distributional impacts suggests that trade liberalization had minor effects on urban poverty, but increased inequality quite considerably. We show that reform-induced impacts on employment and earnings were unequalizing, whereas changes in relative goods prices worked relatively in favor of poorer households. In addition, increasing inequalities were cushioned or exacerbated by factors not related to trade reform. More specifically, we find the following effects and interactions.

- The poverty and distributional effects of increasing informality that can be linked to trade reform appear to be rather small, although the implied increase in inequality and the strong income losses among very poor groups are reasons for concern.
- The increasing unskilled-skilled wage-gap has major negative distributional implications lowering considerably the poverty reduction potential of growth.
- The positive distributional impact of changes in relative prices for consumer goods is relatively strong. The magnitude is comparable to the one of increasing wage inequalities.
- Two factors related to the non-tradable boom, increasing female labor market participation as well as an increase in informal profits, played an important role in cushioning the possible adverse labor market effects of trade liberalization, in particular for the very poor.

The described impacts can be observed in a relatively short time horizon of approximately 5 years. The question of whether trade liberalization is conducive to long-run growth and poverty reduction remains unresolved empirically. Cross-country evidence is inconclusive[42] and in single country studies it is equally difficult to establish causality between trade policy and long-run economic performance. We do not attempt to assess this question for the Colombian case. Yet, the knowledge of medium-term adjustments and their distributional impacts that we have considered in this chapter are important at least for two reasons: First, if trade liberalization leads to increasing inequalities, this increase might well be permanent and socially undesirable.[43] Second, the observed adjustment could provide important insights for designing trade policy reforms, in particular their timing and sequencing, and possible complementary policies.

Colombia already has a very unequal distribution of income. The increase in inequality related to trade liberalization implies that in the future even higher average growth rates will be needed to achieve the same reductions in poverty. Yet, we do not believe that this is reason enough to abandon liberalization altogether. Our analysis has shown that the main source of the inequality increase is not a decline in the incomes of poorer households, but rather a considerable increase in the incomes of the rich. There is hence room for redistributional

---

42 See e.g. Edwards (1998), Rodriguez and Rodrik (2000) and Yanikkaya (2003).
43 Whether this increase has only been temporary, as in the case of Chile (Ferreira and Litchfield 1999), is an interesting question for further research on Colombia.

policies to ensure that the gains of trade liberalization are more equally distributed. We do not think that "static redistribution" through the tax and transfer system is desirable, but suggest that policy-makers should focus on "dynamic redistribution", in particular through the reallocation of resources in education. The guiding principle of educational reform should be to ensure that labor supply can adjust to the increasing wage gap between unskilled and skilled labor, thereby enabling the poorer parts of the population to grasp the opportunities created by trade liberalization.

There are also more general lessons to be learnt from the Colombian experience. One such lesson is that the macroeconomic context matters. In the Colombian case, a thriving domestic economy lowered the adjustment costs of trade liberalization in income distribution terms, as employment creation in non-tradable sectors compensated for employment destruction in import-competing sectors. It is of course unclear whether liberalization would have created jobs in export sectors had there not been a domestic boom associated with a real appreciation. Yet, it is unlikely that these jobs would have been created as fast as jobs in import-competing sectors were destroyed. From a policy perspective, overall domestic economic performance should hence be taken into account when decisions on the speed of liberalization are taken.[44]

---

44 See Falvey and Kim (1992) for a survey of timing and sequencing issues in trade liberalization.

2.6.   Appendices

2.6.1. Additional figures

App. Figure 2.1: Complete growth incidence curves, real data vs. historical simulation 1988-95

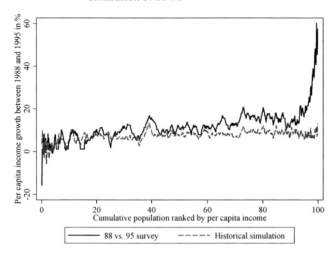

Source: Author's calculations.

App. Figure 2.2: Growth incidence curves, simulations II and III

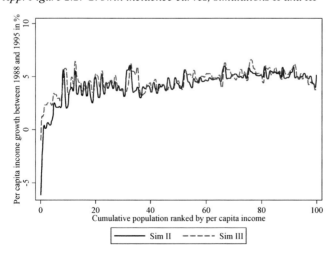

Source: Author's calculations.

App. Figure 2.3: Growth incidence curves, simulations IV and V

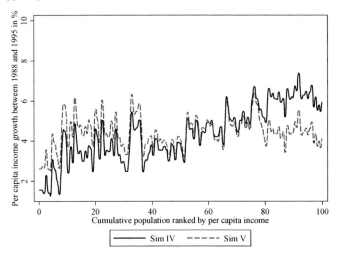

Source: Author's calculations.

2.6.2. Additional tables

App. Table 2.1: Composition of the labor force by gender and skill

	1988	1995
Unskilled Male	43.5	36.8
Skilled Male	21.2	23.9
Unskilled Female	20.9	20.3
Skilled Female	14.4	19.0

Source: Author's calculations.

App. Table 2.2: Estimation results of wage equations and profit function

	Wage				Self-empl.
	unsk male	unsk fem	sk male	unsk fem	income
Years of schooling	0.036	-0.092	0.045	-0.034	
	(0.012)***	-0.105	(0.018)**	-0.134	
Years of schooling squared	0.003	0.009	0.003	0.006	
	(0.001)***	(0.004)**	(0.001)**	-0.005	
Experience	0.047	0.063	0.037	0.045	
	(0.002)***	(0.004)***	(0.004)***	(0.005)***	
Experience squared	-0.001	-0.001	0.000	-0.001	
	(0.000)***	(0.000)***	(0.000)***	(0.000)***	
Education head					0.102
					(0.004)***
Experience head					0.023
					(0.005)***
Experience squared head					0.000
					(0.000)***
Number of self-employed					0.959
					(0.215)***
Constant	9.314	9.956	9.041	9.663	8.656
	(0.050)***	(0.690)***	(0.080)***	(0.877)***	(84.20)**
Observations	6316	3100	2750	2229	4188
R-squared	0.22	0.43	0.18	0.33	0.18

Standard errors in parentheses
* significant at 10%; ** significant at 5%; *** significant at 1%
Note: Regional dummies not reported

App. Table 2.3: Estimation results of the choice models, average marginal effects

	heads			spouses		
	inactive	wage-employed	self-employed	inactive	wage-employed	self-employed
Male	-0.271	0.149	0.123	-0.564	0.423	0.141
	(0.015)***	(0.016)***	(0.013)***	(0.038)***	(0.047)***	(0.058)***
Married	-0.011	0.061	-0.050	-0.019	0.032	-0.014
	-0.008	(0.011)***	(0.010)***	-0.009	(0.011)*	(0.013)***
Years of schooling	0.008	-0.003	-0.005	-0.010	0.021	-0.011
	(0.003)***	-0.005	-0.005	(0.005)**	(0.006)*	(0.007)***
Years of schooling squared	-0.001	0.001	0.000	-0.004	0.003	0.001
	(0.000)***	(0.000)***	0.000	(0.000)***	(0.000)***	(0.000)***
Experience(age-years of schooling-6)	-0.006	-0.004	0.010	0.014	-0.023	0.009
	(0.001)***	(0.002)**	(0.002)***	(0.002)***	(0.001)***	(0.002)***
Experience squared	0.000	0.000	0.000	0.000	0.000	0.000
	(0.000)***	(0.000)*	(0.000)***	(0.000)***	(0.000)***	(0.000)***
Individual other income (source not specified)	0.000	0.000	0.000	0.000	0.000	0.000
	(0.000)***	(0.000)***	(0.000)**	(0.000)**	0.000	0.000
No. of adult males in hh without education	0.017	-0.001	-0.016	0.003	-0.055	0.053
	-0.014	-0.027	-0.024	-0.018	(0.028)*	(0.025)**
No. of adult females in hh without education	0.020	-0.055	0.035	-0.050	-0.010	0.060
	(0.011)*	(0.020)***	(0.019)*	-0.034	(0.036)*	-0.018
No. of adult males in hh with primary education	0.019	-0.003	-0.016	-0.042	-0.013	0.055
	(0.004)***	-0.009	(0.009)*	(0.011)***	(0.007)*	(0.012)***
No. of adult females in hh with primary education	0.005	0.021	-0.026	0.053	-0.002	-0.051
	-0.004	(0.008)**	(0.008)***	(0.012)***	(0.013)***	-0.009
No. of adult males with secondary education	0.015	-0.009	-0.006	-0.041	-0.017	0.058
	(0.003)***	-0.007	-0.006	(0.006)***	(0.009)***	(0.008)***
No. of adult females with secondary education	0.010	0.004	-0.014	-0.002	-0.004	0.006
	(0.003)***	-0.006	(0.006)**	-0.006	-0.009	-0.009
No. of adult males with high education	0.006	-0.010	0.003	0.019	0.007	-0.026
	-0.006	-0.011	-0.011	-0.012	-0.008	(0.010)**
No. of adult females with high education	0.001	-0.015	0.014	-0.002	-0.024	0.026
	-0.005	-0.010	-0.010	(0.013)*	-0.011	(0.016)*
No. of elderly males in hh without education	-0.047	0.132	-0.085	0.075	-0.010	-0.066
	(0.019)**	(0.047)***	(0.042)**	-0.059	-0.067	-0.081
No. of elderly females in hh without education	-0.030	0.010	0.019	0.040	-0.101	0.061
	(0.016)*	-0.033	-0.031	(0.053)*	-0.050	-0.035
No. of elderly males in hh with primary education	-0.026	-0.034	0.060	0.035	-0.031	-0.004
	(0.014)*	-0.027	(0.026)**	-0.023	-0.037	-0.034
No. of elderly females in hh with primary education	0.000	-0.008	0.008	-0.049	0.041	0.008
	-0.008	-0.020	-0.018	(0.024)*	(0.028)*	-0.019
No. of elderly males in hh with high education	-0.037	0.052	-0.015	0.109	-0.067	-0.042
	-0.023	-0.041	-0.036	(0.043)**	(0.039)*	(0.023)*
No. of elderly males with secondary or higher	0.021	-0.077	0.056	0.122	-0.170	0.048
	-0.019	-0.047	-0.044	(0.034)***	(0.066)***	-0.053
No. of children aged 0 to 9	0.002	-0.008	0.006	0.035	-0.004	-0.030
	-0.002	(0.004)**	-0.004	(0.005)***	-0.003	(0.005)***
No. of children aged 10 to 18	-0.004	0.000	0.003	0.002	0.008	-0.010
	-0.002	-0.004	-0.004	(0.005)**	-0.003	-0.005
Wage income of household head				0.000	0.000	0.000
				(0.000)***	0.000	(0.000)***
Observations		12092			8334	
Pseudo R-squared		0.1865			0.0988	

	inactive	others wage-employed	self-employed
Male	0.237 (0.012)***	-0.320 (0.008)***	0.083 (0.011)***
Married	-0.005 -0.012	0.130 (0.018)***	-0.125 (0.020)***
Years of schooling	-0.013 (0.007)*	0.012 (0.006)**	0.001 -0.004
Years of schooling squared	0.000 0.000	-0.001 (0.000)**	0.001 (0.000)**
Experience(age-years of schooling-6)	0.011 (0.002)***	0.019 (0.002)***	-0.030 (0.001)***
Experience squared	0.001 (0.000)***	0.000 (0.000)***	0.000 (0.000)***
Individual other income (source not specified)	0.000 0.000	0.000 (0.000)***	0.000 (0.000)***
No. of adult males in hh without education	-0.012 -0.013	-0.007 -0.022	0.019 -0.019
No. of adult females in hh without education	0.006 -0.019	0.002 -0.020	-0.007 -0.012
No. of adult males in hh with primary education	0.025 (0.007)**	-0.018 -0.004	-0.007 (0.006)***
No. of adult females in hh with primary education	0.006 (0.005)***	0.014 (0.008)*	-0.021 -0.007
No. of adult males with secondary education	-0.006 (0.006)***	-0.026 -0.005	0.032 (0.006)***
No. of adult females with secondary education	0.015 (0.004)***	0.000 -0.005	-0.015 (0.006)**
No. of adult males with high education	0.005 (0.011)***	-0.040 (0.011)***	0.035 -0.008
No. of adult females with high education	-0.039 -0.007	0.032 (0.011)***	0.007 (0.011)***
No. of elderly males in hh without education	-0.075 -0.041	0.035 (0.013)***	0.040 -0.039
No. of elderly females in hh without education	-0.012 -0.037	-0.011 -0.023	0.023 -0.032
No. of elderly males in hh with primary education	0.032 -0.025	0.016 (0.027)*	-0.048 -0.016
No. of elderly females in hh with primary education	-0.016 -0.018	0.001 -0.020	0.015 -0.012
No. of elderly males in hh with high education	-0.004 -0.040	-0.005 -0.027	0.010 -0.041
No. of elderly males with secondary or higher	-0.096 -0.029	0.010 (0.042)**	0.086 (0.047)*
No. of children aged 0 to 9	0.009 (0.003)*	0.006 (0.005)***	-0.014 (0.004)**
No. of children aged 10 to 18	0.001 (0.003)**	0.006 -0.004	-0.007 (0.004)*
Wage income of household head	0.000 0.000	0.000 (0.000)**	0.000 (0.000)***
Observations	9303		
Pseudo R-squared	0.1345		

Standard errors in parentheses
* significant at 10%; ** significant at 5%; *** significant at 1%

App. Table 2.4:   Percentage point changes in sectoral employment composition,
                  urban labor force, 1988-95

| | unskilled male | | skilled male | | unskilled female | | skilled female | | | Total | |
	wage	self	wage	self	wage	self	wage	self	wage	self	all
agr	-0.6	-0.2	-0.6	1.0	-0.4	0.1	-0.1	0.0	-0.5	0.1	-0.4
min	-0.1	-0.2	-0.1	0.4	0.0	0.1	-0.1	-0.7	-0.1	-0.1	-0.1
light man	-0.3	0.7	-0.3	-0.6	-0.1	-4.2	-0.2	-1.9	-0.9	-0.6	-0.9
heav man	-1.0	0.7	-0.3	0.7	-2.2	0.3	1.0	1.2	-1.0	0.7	-0.7
util	-0.2		0.2		0.1		-0.6		-0.1		-0.1
const	1.1	9.1	1.1	4.5	0.5	0.1	0.1	0.7	-0.1	4.4	1.2
trade rest	0.8	-5.8	2.8	-7.1	-0.8	0.5	2.0	1.8	1.5	-3.4	0.8
trans	0.6	3.4	-0.3	9.1	0.0	0.1	-0.5	0.2	-0.4	2.7	0.6
comm	0.3		0.5		0.2		0.1		0.4		0.2
fin	0.8	0.4	-2.4	-1.8	-1.1	0.2	-0.9	-3.7	-0.1	0.3	-0.2
pub	-2.0		-0.9		-0.2		-0.8		-0.8		-0.7
oth serv	0.6	-8.1	0.3	-6.2	4.1	2.7	-0.2	2.4	2.1	-4.2	0.3

Source: Author's calculations.

App. Table 2.5:   Shares of manufacturing wage-employment across labor market
                  segments

	1988	1995	point diff
Unskilled Male	21.6	18.8	-2.9
Skilled Male	20.1	18.9	-1.2
Unskilled Female	23.4	20.0	-3.3
Skilled Female	14.5	14.6	0.0
Total Urban	20.7	18.3	-2.4

Source: Author's calculations.

App. Table 2.6:   Sectoral shares of wage-employment and skill intensity (wage-
                  employment, 1988 and 1995

| | Share in employment | | Skilled labor share | | % point | |
	1988	1995	1988	1995	diff.	% diff.
agr	1.7	1.2	30.0	36.8	6.8	22.6
min	0.5	0.4	47.1	54.8	7.7	16.4
light man	17.3	16.4	28.4	35.6	7.2	25.4
heav man	10.5	9.5	34.8	47.1	12.3	35.4
util	1.2	1.1	53.9	63.3	9.4	17.5
const	6.8	6.7	16.8	24.8	8.1	48.3
trade rest	20.3	21.8	39.5	50.6	11.1	28.0
trans	5.8	5.4	28.1	32.8	4.8	17.0
comm	0.6	0.9	70.7	71.1	0.4	0.6
fin	8.7	8.5	61.6	66.1	4.6	7.4
pub	5.4	4.6	61.8	78.2	16.4	26.5
oth serv	21.4	23.5	48.1	54.7	6.6	13.8
Total	100.0	100.0	40.0	48.9	8.8	22.0

Source: Author's calculations.

3. Resource booms, inequality, and poverty: The case of gas in Bolivia

3.1. Introduction

In principle, countries richly endowed with natural resources, may it be fertile soils or mineral resources, should be able to prosper and overcome poverty faster than resource-poor countries. Yet, the experience of many resource-rich countries illustrates that this is not necessarily the case. Often, resource-rich countries go through boom and bust cycles that finally leave them poorer than resource-poor countries with similar initial conditions. Through a number of different channels resource wealth may negatively affect economic development.[45] In many instances, tradable sectors become uncompetitive and shrink excessively because export revenues are consumed quickly rather than invested. This can be particularly harmful for economic development, as these sectors, especially manufacturing, are believed to exhibit important positive externalities, whereas resource sectors are often said to have an enclave character with few spillovers to the rest of the economy. In addition to hampering economic development, wealth and income in resource-dependent economies tend to be distributed very unequally, as resource rents typically benefit a small privileged group. As a more unequal distribution of income results in a lower rate of poverty reduction for a given growth rate, it is therefore unlikely that resource-rich countries achieve pro-poor growth, i.e. a growth pattern from which the poor benefit disproportionately, without deliberate interventions in favor of the poor.

There is an extensive empirical literature on the "resource curse" and the channels through which it operates. Starting with Sachs and Warner (1997), many authors have confirmed that resource-rich countries actually grow more slowly than resource-poor countries using cross-country growth regressions. Yet, the impact of resource booms (and busts) on economic development and poverty as well as the transmission channels depend on both country and resource characteristics. Therefore, quite some country case studies have been undertaken, which have sharpened our understanding of how the resource curse works. Some of these studies, for example the collection in Auty (2001), have focused on the impact of resource wealth on long-term development, whereas other studies have rather looked at the short to medium run economic impact of a resource boom or bust. The studies in Gelb et al. (1988) examine the economic impact of the oil windfalls in the late 1970s on a number of oil-exporting developing economies. These case studies focus on relative price effects, related sectoral shifts, in particular the performance of agriculture, and the fiscal response, especially public investment programs. The case studies included in Collier and Gunning (1999a and 1999b) centre on the savings response of public and private agents when faced with trade shocks.

---

45 See Auty (2001) and Lay and Omar Mahmoud (2004) for surveys of the literature on the resource curse.

The present chapter examines one particular resource shock, namely the gas boom Bolivia experienced in the late 1990s and early 2000s. Following the studies in Gelb et al. (1988), we analyze the sectoral shifts and the fiscal response to the gas shock in the short to medium run. In contrast to these studies, our focus is on the poverty and distributional effects of the shock. We consider some of our findings to be of relevance to poor resource-rich countries with similar structural characteristics. The central question is whether the gas boom really bypasses large parts of the (poor) population in Bolivia, thereby leading to increasing inequalities in an already very unequal society. We examine the transmission channels through which the large resource inflows related to the gas boom, both initial foreign investment in the sector and the subsequent export earnings, as well as large public transfer programs (that may well be interpreted as a means of redistributing resource rents) affect the distribution of income. In doing so, we focus on general equilibrium effects and the corresponding labor market impacts, in particular on shifts in formal vs. informal employment and changes in relative factor prices. These transmission channels seem to be particularly relevant, as direct employment effects of the resource boom are virtually absent.

To address these issues adequately, we propose a modeling framework that captures the structural features of the Bolivian economy and allows us to trace the poverty and distributional implications of the resource-boom-induced changes on the labor market. The framework therefore consists of a multi-sectoral computable general equilibrium (CGE) model that is combined with a microsimulation model. The CGE model allows us to construct counterfactual scenarios to disentangle the effects of the gas boom from other shocks that the Bolivian economy experienced at the same time and to trace the transmission channels at work at the macroeconomic level. Changes in important factor market aggregates from the CGE model, more specifically changes in relative factor prices and in the workforce composition in terms of formal and informal sector employment, are then passed on to a microsimulation model. The microsimulation model is based on an income generation model estimated on household survey data and produces a counterfactual income distribution given the CGE model results.

The remainder of the chapter is structured as follows. The first part provides an overview of the scope and scale of the gas boom that began to shape the Bolivian economy in the late 1990s and a first broad assessment of its macroeconomic impact. It also motivates the counterfactual simulations of the second part. There, we first describe our methodological framework and then present our results. The final section concludes.

3.2. The gas boom and other resource shocks

We consider Bolivia a particularly interesting case for the following reasons. It is the poorest country of South America with a long history of resource-induced booms and busts, and quite some observers have argued that the country's resource wealth is the root cause of its poverty (e.g. Auty and Evia 2001). The structural reforms of the 1980s and 1990s have been associated with some growth, but that growth has not done the job of lifting large parts of the population out of poverty in an economy with a highly unequal distribution of income, although poverty has been reduced somewhat in the course of the 1990s.

Bolivia's economy has always been and still is highly dependent on natural resources. In the 1990s, hydrocarbons and minerals have typically accounted for roughly 50 percent of exports and the hydrocarbons sector contributes significantly to public revenues. In the second half of the 1990s, huge investments have been undertaken in the gas sector to explore and exploit Bolivia's vast gas reserves. Recent reserve additions have turned Bolivia into the second largest gas reserve holder in Latin America only after Venezuela. A new gas pipeline to Brazil went into operation in 1999 through which the bulk of Bolivia's gas exports run today, and gas exports are expected to increase further in the following years.

The gas shock can be split into three important components: first, the huge investment into the gas sector between 1997 and 2003, most of which was foreign direct investment; second, the gas exports through the new pipeline to Brazil; and third, the government take of the gas rents. Figure 1 illustrates the magnitude of these components as a share of GDP in the 1990s. Investments in the gas sector reached about 10 percent of GDP in the peak years 1998 and 1999. Unfortunately, more recent figures beyond 2001 are not available. Figure 3.1 also shows the phasing out of gas exports to Argentina in the course of the 1990s and the gas exports to Brazil, which started in 1999. By 2003, gas exports to Brazil accounted for almost 8 percent of GDP, as they had reached the contracted volume, which under the current contract is going to be roughly constant until 2019. In addition, gas exports to Argentina are likely to rise again, as new contracts were signed in 2005. Exports will thus mainly fluctuate due to fluctuations in gas prices, which are linked to a basket of international energy prices.[46] Numbers on the government take from the gas sector are difficult to obtain. Here, we draw on a study by the Energy Sector Management Assistance Programme (ESMAP) (2002) of UNDP and World Bank, which places the government take in 2001 at more than 4 percent of GDP. According to the Ley de Hidrocarburos from 1996, the government take comprises royalties, a profit tax and a tax on remittances abroad, which is why the government take cannot be easily calculated from publicly available budgetary publications.

---

46 This of course only holds if both Brazil and Bolivia comply with the signed contract.

Figure 3.1: Major gas-related resource flows in percent of GDP, 1990-2003

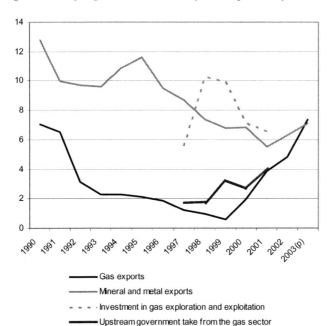

——— Gas exports

———— Mineral and metal exports

- - - Investment in gas exploration and exploitation

——— Upstream government take from the gas sector

Source: Authors' calculations.

Note: Data on GDP, exports, and investment in gas exploration and exploitation from
INE. Upstream government take from the gas sector is from a study of the joint
UNDP/World Bank Energy Sector Management Assistance Programme (ESMAP)
(2002). The government take includes royalties, patents, and taxes on profits. Values
for 2003 are preliminary.

The gas boom was arguably the biggest but not the only significant external
shock. The Bolivian economy was hit by an adverse terms of trade shock in the
late 1990s, which comprised falling prices for exports of the four major metals
zinc, gold, tin and silver. These shocks together with a further expansion of
soybean production in the Bolivian lowlands had a major impact on the
composition of Bolivian exports in the second half of the 1990s and the early
2000s (Figure 3.2). Hydrocarbon exports rose steeply from less than 10 percent to
more than 30 percent of total exports over the period 1999-2004, as did soy and
soy derivatives exports from 5 percent in 1990 to more than 20 percent in 2004.
By contrast, exports of minerals and metals experienced quite some decline from
well above 40 percent in the early 1990s to about 20 percent in 2004. On balance,
the already high degree of export concentration increased even further. By 2004,
the three product groups accounted for 80 percent of Bolivia's exports.

Figure 3.2: Composition of exports in percent, 1990-2004

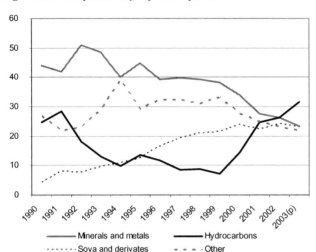

Source: Data from UDAPE Dossier Vol. 15 (2005).

Note: Values for 2004 are preliminary.

The resource shocks were associated with substantial macroeconomic adjustments. Figure 3.3 shows the real effective exchange rate and some major balance-of-payments items for the 1990s and the early 2000s. After a real depreciation in the early 1990s, Bolivia experienced a strong appreciation following the inflow of foreign direct investment that was mainly directed at the gas sector. There are thus clear signs of Dutch disease effects in the second half of the 1990s, which appear to dominate the impact of the negative commodity price shock. The current account deteriorated until 1999, imports increased and exports fell. Only after 2000, exports started to recover, led by rising gas deliveries to Brazil. The dramatic decrease in exports in the second half of the 1990s can of course not entirely be attributed to the export sectors loosing competitiveness because of real exchange rate appreciation. Another important factor were the commodity price shocks for Bolivia's major exported metals. In addition, the Brazilian crisis from 1999 negatively affected Bolivia's export demand, all the more so as the trigger of the crisis was a massive devaluation of the Brazilian Real.

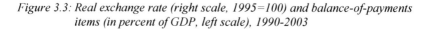

*Figure 3.3: Real exchange rate (right scale, 1995=100) and balance-of-payments
items (in percent of GDP, left scale), 1990-2003*

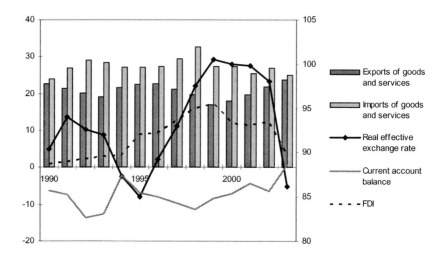

Source: Data from IMF International Financial Statistics (March 2005).

The gas boom and other external shocks also had some impact on sectoral
growth rates in the second half of the 1990s. When studying the Bolivian national
accounts, one will find that the gas boom after 1996 appears to have triggered a
tremendous construction boom. Yet, according to personal correspondence with
INE, these figures reflect the construction of the gas pipeline to Brazil with the
bulk of pipeline-related construction works entering the national accounts in 1998.
When pipeline construction is deducted, there are still signs of a temporary, yet
less pronounced increase in construction activities in the late 1990s (App. Figure
3.1). As Figure 3.4 indicates, overall sectoral change in the 1990s has been
modest; there are, however, some indications of Dutch disease type adjustments.
The most important non-tradable sector, the services sector, seems to have
benefited from the gas boom, as it grew significantly stronger after 1996. Starting
from a very low base, modern agriculture, one of the most export-oriented sectors,
expanded very strongly in the 1990s, while traditional agriculture experienced the
lowest growth rates, its importance therefore declining. The main factor behind the
drop in modern agriculture's share after 1997 is arguably not the gas boom and the
associated real appreciation, but rather the 1997/98 El Niño, which caused planted
soybean areas to contract.

Figure 3.4: Sectoral shares in GDP, 1992-1997-2001

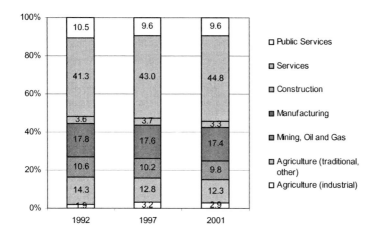

Source: Data from INE (www.ine.gov.bo, 2005).

As regards changes in employment, in particular shifts between formal and informal employment, there is strong evidence of increasing informality in the late 1990s in Bolivia. Spatz (2004a) finds a drop in the formal sector share from 55 percent in 1997 to only 50 percent in 2001. Using different data and a slightly different definition of the informal sector, Tannuri-Pianto et al. (2004) detect an even more pronounced decrease in formal employment (from 44 percent in 1997 to 32 percent in 2002). Klasen et al. (2006) stress the importance of tight labor market regulations in the presence of negative external shocks as the root cause of increasing informality.

The preceding analysis suggests that the gas boom provided substantial (additional) fiscal resources to the Bolivian government. A key question is whether these resources have been directed towards the poorer parts of the population. Possibly somewhat surprisingly, the Bolivian fiscal stance deteriorated during the period under investigation despite these additional resources. In 2003, the overall budget deficit amounted to 8 percent of GDP. The root cause of the fiscal problems is what many observers have perceived as a failed pension reform that dates back to 1996. It should be noted that pension payments out of the old pay-as-you-go system in Bolivia represent a highly regressive transfer, as they cover 2 percent of the Bolivian population at the incredible cost of 5 percent of GDP (World Bank 2004).

Increased spending on social security left little room for raising expenditure targeted at the poorer parts of the population. Nevertheless, pro-poor expenditure in basic social services, defined as expenditure in primary and secondary education, primary health care, and the Bonosol[47] payment, increased from 9.1 (27) to 12.4 (33) percent of GDP (total public expenditure) between 1995 and 2002. It should however be taken into account that about half of Bolivia's basic social expenditure is funded by donors and official loans. Studying the effectiveness of these expenditure shifts goes beyond the scope of this chapter.

Yet, the increasing share of pension payments certainly represents the major public expenditure shift that can be observed during the period under investigation. It may be seen as a consequence of bad fiscal management and a badly implemented reform. We are however inclined to interpret this expenditure shift as being related to the expectation of the windfall profits from gas exports and hence as a way to transfer resource rents to the population – although this interpretation is of course open to debate.

3.3. The modelling framework

Having established that resource shocks, and in particular the gas boom, were associated with major adjustments in the Bolivian economy, we now turn to a counterfactual analysis in which we examine the isolated impact of the gas boom. In the analysis, we combine a CGE model with a microsimulation model, connecting the two through several link variables.

3.3.1. The CGE model

The CGE model provides a standard recursive-dynamic, trade-focused representation of the national economy.[48] However, to make it applicable for the analysis of the gas boom, the model differs from the typical specification in two important respects: first, production is split up into formal and informal activities. Such a distinction enables us to examine one possible channel through which the gas boom and the associated real appreciation might have had a negative distributional impact, namely by forcing workers to switch from more productive formal activities to less productive informal activities. This mechanism is similar in spirit to those assumed in much of the literature on the resource curse. Sachs and Warner (1995), for example, argue that resource booms tend to be detrimental to economic growth as Dutch disease effects lead to a contraction of sectors exhibiting positive externalities. Second, exploration and pipeline construction are

---

47 The Bonosol payment was introduced in the late 1990s as an annuity to be paid to every Bolivian aged 65 or more out of the proceeds of privatization. The first payment of US$ 212 was made in 1997. The government however soon realized that such an amount would not be sustainable and reduced the annual payment to US$ 60 (under a new name "Bolivida"). Bolivida payments however were not processed until 2001. Political pressure led the Sanchez de Lozada administration to reinstitute the Bonosol payment of US$ 240 in 2003. See Escobar and Nina (2004) and Martinez (2004) for details.

48 Van der Mensbrugghe (2003) gives a technical description of the prototype CGE model on which our model is based.

considered as separate investment demand categories in order to model the huge investment outlays that preceded the expansion of the gas sector.

On the production side, the model differentiates between activities and commodities, thus allowing for the same commodity to be produced by one or more sectors, and for the same sector to produce one or more commodities. To take just one example, the modern agricultural sector does not only grow cash crops such as soybeans, but is also engaged in livestock farming. Sectoral output results from combining intermediate goods and six different primary factors (skilled labor, unskilled labor, formal capital, informal capital, land, and a sector-specific resource in the case of oil and gas) in a nested CES structure.[49] International trade is specified along conventional lines, with import demand being derived from a CES aggregation function of domestic and imported goods, and export supply from a Constant Elasticity of Transformation (CET) function of domestically sold and exported goods. Export demand is infinitely elastic, i.e., the small-country assumption holds.

The disaggregation of production, which is based on a Social Accounting Matrix (SAM) for 2001, reveals structural differences between formal and informal operations, even though they are not as clear-cut as theoretical models tend to suggest (Table 3.1). Regarding trade orientation, the sectors with the highest trade shares are all formal, but since several other formal sectors produce pure non-traded goods, we can only tentatively hypothesize that the gas boom has led to an informalization of the economy via Dutch disease effects. A more pronounced pattern emerges with respect to the composition of factor income. It turns out that all informal activities make intensive use of unskilled labor, whereas capital intensity is high in most formal activities.

The sectoral composition of value added reflects certain assumptions about how factor markets operate. We distinguish two categories of capital that are specific to formal and informal activities, respectively. Formal (informal) capital is partially mobile within the formal (informal) economy, which is modeled by means of CET functions. By contrast, our specification does not allow land to be shifted between modern and traditional agriculture given that the two activities are regionally separated.[50] The natural resource is sector-specific; its supply is a positive function of the resource price relative to the economy-wide price level. The market for unskilled labor is segmented between rural and urban areas, where modern agriculture is considered part of the urban economy, as it resembles other (formal) urban activities in using wage labor and capital rather than relying on self-employment. The two segments are linked through rural-urban migration. Along the lines of the Harris-Todaro model, the decision to migrate depends on wage differentials. Skilled labor is assumed to be fully mobile across production sectors. Market clearing is achieved via wage adjustments, but the intersectoral

---

49 For the exact nesting structure, see van der Mensbrugghe (2003).

50 Note that the model allows for both limiting cases – perfect capital (land) mobility and perfect capital (land) immobility – as well as any intermediate case due to the CET specification.

wage differentials observed in the base period are assumed to persist. These differentials point to systematically lower labor productivity in informal sectors. Unskilled workers, for example, receive only slightly more than half the average wage in the informal construction sector, while they are almost paid the average wage in the formal sector (Table 3.2).

Table 3.1: Structural Characteristics of the Bolivian Economy

Sectors	Trade orientation		Factor income as share of value added					
	Imports	Exports	LabU	LabS	KapInf	KapForm	LandR	NatRs
TradAgr	0.07	0.02	0.67				0.33	
ForFis		0.09	0.56	0.33		0.02		0.09
Formal								
ModAgr	0.09	0.16	0.20	0.27		0.25	0.28	
OilGas		0.31		0.11		0.31		0.58
Exploration				0.09		0.91		
FoodPro	0.07	0.14	0.26	0.23		0.50		
OthLiMan	0.20	0.14	0.34	0.36		0.30		
Chem	0.53	0.02	0.35	0.05		0.60		
OilRef	0.12	0.02	0.02	0.10		0.88		
Min	0.11	0.37	0.18	0.09		0.73		
HeavMan	0.60	0.20	0.51	0.27		0.22		
EleGasWat			0.01	0.16		0.82		
Const			0.30	0.28		0.43		
Trade			0.17	0.33		0.50		
Trans	0.06	0.05	0.37	0.27		0.36		
CommFinBus	0.04	0.03	0.03	0.27		0.70		
RealEst						1.00		
SocPerServ	0.02	0.01	0.13	0.37		0.50		
HotRest	0.05	0.05	0.31	0.21		0.48		
PubServ			0.07	0.93				
Informal								
FoodPro	0.07	0.15	0.50	0.20	0.30			
OthLiMan	0.20	0.14	0.51	0.19	0.30			
Const			0.55	0.09	0.36			
TradeDomS			0.49	0.21	0.30			
Trans	0.06	0.05	0.43	0.20	0.36			
HotRest	0.05	0.05	0.44	0.10	0.46			

Imports as share of absorption plus intermediate demand
Exports as share of total production

Source: Authors' calculations based on the Social Accounting Matrix for 2001.

Note: Imports are calculated as a share of absorption, exports as a share of domestic production.

Table 3.2: Sectoral Deviations from average wages

Sectors	Skilled labor		Unskilled labor	
	Formal	Informal	Formal	Informal
Food Pro	2.85	1.27	3.26	2.57
OthLiMan	0.65	0.38	1.31	0.94
Const	0.65	0.29	0.97	0.54
Trade	0.42	0.27	0.50	0.49
Trans	1.67	1.03	3.72	2.30
Hot Rest	0.59	0.33	1.15	0.70

Source: Authors' calculations.

Note: A value above (below) one indicates higher-than-average (lower-than-average) wages. Computed from the SAM.

The factor income generated in the production process is distributed to four different household groups – poor and rich urban households as well as poor and rich rural households – according to fixed coefficients derived from the SAM. Moreover, households receive transfers in fixed proportions to government expenditures and remittances from abroad that are fixed in foreign currency. They use their gross income to pay taxes, to save and to consume. The allocation of consumption expenditures on different goods is modeled employing a Linear Expenditure System (LES). The sectoral allocation of government and the non-gas component of investment demand are both governed by fixed coefficients, whereas investment demand for exploration and pipeline construction is exogenously given.

Despite the exogeneity of gas-related investment, the model is savings-driven, i.e., non-gas investment adjusts so as to bring about the necessary ex-post identity of savings and investment. The balance of payments equilibrium is determined by the equality of exogenous foreign savings to the value of the current account. With fixed world prices, the real exchange rate serves as the equilibrating variable. In the macro closure for the government, the budget deficit is allowed to adjust in order to achieve a predetermined level of real government expenditures at a fixed household income tax schedule.

A simple recursive-dynamic framework allows us to implement the gas boom as a sequence of shocks (see below) and to trace over time the changes in economic structure caused by the boom. There are four elements driving model dynamics – exogenous labor growth, investment-driven capital accumulation, exogenous growth of natural resources in the gas sector, and exogenous productivity growth. Several other exogenous variables require updating to arrive at a realistic baseline scenario. Government expenditures and transfers, for example, are assumed to grow at the same rate as GDP.

Finally, the CGE model is linked to the microsimulation model. We assume that the link is sequential, i.e., the CGE model is solved first and certain target values are passed to the microsimulation that is "forced" to reproduce the aggregate changes in these targets. In line with our focus on skilled vs. unskilled labor and formal vs. informal employment, the following link variables are used: (1) the share of unskilled workers in the formal sector, (2) share of skilled workers in the formal sector, (3) mean wages for skilled workers, (4) mean wages for unskilled workers, and (5) mean informal profits.[51] While the first four link variables have a straightforward interpretation, the fifth is based on the concept of mixed income received by self-employed workers. Accordingly, informal profits are calculated as the sum of skilled and unskilled labor income as well as informal capital income.

Before we discuss the specification of the microsimulation model, it should be stressed that the CGE and the microsimulation model should not be seen as a consistent macro-micro modelling framework. Rather, the idea of combining these two types of simulation models in a sequential fashion is to get "the best of the two modeling worlds". The CGE model is a useful tool to examine the transmission channels of the resource boom. It provides a consistent modeling framework based on an empirical representation of the Bolivian economy and yields a numerical counterfactual approximation of the shocks' labor market impacts. Yet, in order to assess the ultimate poverty and distributional consequences of the shocks, the microsimulation is a much more suitable tool. It takes into account household heterogeneity in terms of factor endowments at a much more detailed level and models occupational choices and corresponding earnings changes at the individual level. Sequentially combining these models typically implies the imposition of a number of ad-hoc assumptions that may not be satisfying from a theoretical perspective.

3.3.2. The microsimulation model

The microsimulation model is based on an income generation model that is estimated on household survey data.[52] The following estimations are based on all individuals employed outside traditional agriculture, as our focus is on changes in

---

51 Although formal profits account for an important share in value added, they are not passed to the microsimulation for two reasons. First, most formal profits are retained and invested. Second, capital income is likely to be measured very poorly in household surveys. As formal profits increase considerably during the gas boom, we may systematically ignore an inequality-increasing factor.

52 We use the Encuesta Continua de Hogares from 2001. The survey comprises 24 996 individuals from 5 797 households. Due to a number of missing income observations, incomes were imputed based on income equations estimated separately by labor market segments (smallholder, worker in traditional agriculture, agricultural employer, worker in modern agriculture, informal self-employed/employer, informal worker, formal employer, and formal worker). This imputation is also necessary for using income data for poverty and distributional analysis.

formal vs. informal employment. In contrast to the CGE model, the microsimulation hence assumes that smallholders remain in their occupation.[53]

The two basic components of this income generation model are a model of occupational choices that represents the "choice" between formal and informal employment[54] as well as earnings functions that correspond to the respective sector of employment. If individuals happen to be in (or switch to) the formal sector they are assumed to earn a wage, whereas individuals in the informal sector are assumed to be (or become) part of a household enterprise and contribute to the profits earned by this enterprise. Table 3.3 provides an overview of the equations of the income generation model, the econometric models, the sub-samples and lists of the explanatory variables. We limit the discussion of the specification to innovative and interesting features. As estimation results correspond to expectations, we do not further comment them here, but report the detailed results in App. Table 3.1 and App. Table 3.2.

The choice between informal and formal activities is estimated separately for household heads, spouses, and other household members using a logit model. The equations of the choice model are interrelated through the head's wage (and hence her choice) entering the occupational choice model of spouses and other household members. We hence assume a sequential choice with the household head deciding first.

In addition to the formal-informal segmentation, we assume segmentation according to skill levels, differentiating between unskilled and skilled labor (defined in terms of years of schooling). We therefore estimate separate wage equations for skilled and the unskilled labor employed in the formal sector using OLS. The set of explanatory variables (reported in Table 3.3) is standard. The individuals in the informal sector are assumed to pool resources and work effort in a household enterprise, for which we estimate a profit function. The numbers of informal unskilled as well as informal skilled individuals enter as separate explanatory variables. As the number of household members working in the enterprise is very likely to depend on the prospective profits to be earned in informal activities, we are likely to have an endogeneity problem here. We therefore instrument the number of unskilled as well as skilled household enterprise members. As instruments we use the total number of (informal and formal) household members (unskilled or skilled, respectively, that we additionally

---

53 The income generation model is based on a model first proposed by Alatas and Bourguignon (2005) to decompose inequality and poverty changes between two household surveys. See Bourguignon, Ferreira, and Lustig (2005a) for a selection of country studies using this type of decomposition technique. It has also been used in a macro-micro simulation framework by Robilliard et al. (2002) and Bussolo and Lay (2005).

54 Employment is assumed to be informal if the individual is self-employed/non-remunerated household member and/or works in an enterprise with less than 5 employees.

differentiate by gender and age) interacted with the share of formal employment of the province of residence.

Table 3.3: Overview of the income generation model

	Explained variable and estimated equation	Model	Sub-sample	Explanatory variables
1	Being in formal or informal sector $P(formal = 1 \mid X^h) = g(c^h + X^h\alpha^h)$	Logit	Heads	Education (squared), experience, female, share of formal workers in province of residence
2	Being in formal or informal sector $P(formal = 1 \mid X^s) = g(c^s + X^s\alpha^s)$	Logit	Spouses	Education (squared), experience, female, indigenous, geographical dummies, number of children under 10 (interacted with female), share of formal workers in province of residence, log wage of household head (if head formal)
3	Being in formal or informal sector $P(formal = 1 \mid X^O) = g(c^O + X^O\alpha^O)$	Logit	Others	Education (squared), experience, female, widow, number of children under 10 (interacted with female), share of formal workers in province of residence, log wage of household head (if head formal)
4	Unskilled wage $\ln w^{us} = c^{us} + X^{us}\beta^{us} + uw^{us}$	Linear	Unskilled formal sector	Education (squared), experience (squared), female, geographical dummies
5	Skilled wage $\ln w^{sk} = c^{sk} + X^{sk}\beta^{sk} + uw^{sk}$	Linear	Skilled formal sector	
6	Profits of household enterprise $\ln p = c^p + X^p\beta^p + up$	Linear	Informal sector enterprises (max. one per household)	Average education of members (squared), Average experience of members (squared), number of female members, geographical dummies, *number of members*

These estimated relationships form the basis of the microsimulation. The microsimulation is shocked using changes in the five link variables that are passed on from the CGE analysis. To gain an understanding of how the microsimulation works it is useful to think of the set of equations summarized in Table 3.3 as a system of equations.

Let employment n be the sum of n^{us} and n^{sk}, the number of unskilled and skilled labor, respectively.

$n^{us} + n^{sk} = n$

fs^{us} denotes the formal share of employment among the unskilled. The number of formal unskilled nf^{us} is given by the sum of heads, spouses, and other household members that derive a higher "utility" from being employed in the formal than from being employed in the informal sector where ($ind_{us\_h}(\hat{c}^h + X^h\hat{\alpha}^h + uh1 > uh0)$) is an indicator function assuming 1 if the condition in brackets is fulfilled and 0 otherwise. $uh0, uh1, us0, us1, uo0, uo1$ are residuals for heads, spouses, and others, respectively, that cannot be observed in latent variable models and are hence drawn consistent with the observed choice.[55]

$$fs^{us} = \frac{nf^{us}}{n^{us}} \quad \frac{\sum_{us\_h} ind_{us\_h}(\hat{c}^h + X^h\hat{\alpha}^h + uh1 > uh0) + \sum_{us\_s} ind_{us\_s}(\hat{c}^s + X^s\hat{\alpha}^s + us1 > us1)}{+ \sum_{us\_o} ind_{us\_o}(\hat{c}^o + X^o\hat{\alpha}^o + uo1 > uo0) = nf^{us}} \quad (1)$$

We have the same set of equations for skilled labor (2).

$$fs^{sk} = \frac{nf^{sk}}{n^{sk}} \quad \frac{\sum_{sk\_h} ind_{sk\_h}(\hat{c}^h + X^h\hat{\alpha}^h + uh1 > uh0) + \sum_{sk\_s} ind_{sk\_s}(\hat{c}^s + X^s\hat{\alpha}^s + us1 > us1)}{+ \sum_{sk\_o} ind_{sk\_o}(\hat{c}^o + X^o\hat{\alpha}^o + uo1 > uo0) = nf^{sk}} \quad (2)$$

The mean unskilled wage is the wage of all unskilled workers in the formal sector divided by the number of unskilled formal workers.

$$mean(w^{us}) = \frac{\sum_{us\_h} ind_{us\_h}(..)w^{us}_{us\_h} + \sum_{us\_s} ind_{us\_s}(..)ws^{us}_{us\_s} + \sum_{us\_o} ind_{us\_o}(..)w^{us}_{us\_s}}{nf^{us}} \quad (3)$$

where $w^{us} = \exp(\hat{c}^{us} + X^{us}\hat{\beta}^{us} + \hat{u}w^{us})$ is the individual unskilled wage with $\hat{u}w^{us}$, the observed residual. The same equation holds for the skilled

$$mean(w^{sk}) = \frac{\sum_{sk\_h} ind_{sk\_h}(..)w^{sk}_{sk\_h} + \sum_{sk\_s} ind_{sk\_s}(..)ws^{sk}_{sk\_s} + \sum_{sk\_o} ind_{sk\_o}(..)w^{sk}_{sk\_s}}{nf^{sk}} \quad (4)$$

where $w^{sk} = \exp(\hat{c}^{sk} + X^{sk}\hat{\beta}^{sk} + \hat{u}w^{sk})$.

Whereas wages are summed over individuals, total profits from informal activities are summed over households (hh)

---

55   Residuals are drawn conditional on the observed choice, as suggested by Bourguignon, Fournier, and Gurgand (1998). We randomly draw two residuals from a Gumbel distribution (type I extreme value, variance $\pi^2/6$), one for each alternative. This is equivalent to drawing one logistically distributed residual, as the difference of two Gumbel-distributed random variables is logistically distributed (with variance $\pi^2/3$). See Train (2003) for details.

$$mean(p) = \frac{\sum_{hh} p_{hh}}{n - nf^{us} - nf^{sk}}$$ (5)

where the profit p_{hh} in household *hh* will only be greater than 0 if at least one member is employed in the informal sector.

$$p_{hh} = \exp(\hat{c}^p + X^p \hat{\beta}^p + \hat{u}p)(-1)\left[(ind_h(..)-1) + (ind_s(..)-1) + \sum_o (ind_o(..)-1) \right]$$ (6)

Remember also that the number of (skilled and unskilled) household enterprise members enters the profit function.

$$X^p = f\left(ind_h(..); ind_s(..); \sum_o ind_o(..) \right)$$ (7)

The above equations describe the initial distribution of labor income (with the exception of traditional agriculture). As mentioned above, the microsimulation is "forced" to reproduce the changes in the aggregates given by the CGE model. This is achieved by varying the constants in the above system of equations such that the household income generation model just reproduces the target values. Increasing e.g. the constant $\hat{c}^h$ leads some heads to switch from informal to formal activities. When individuals switch from informal to formal activities, they are assigned a simulated wage residual, as we do not have an observed unexplained wage $\hat{u}w$ for her. The same holds if an individual becomes the first household member active in the informal sector (not if she joins an existing enterprise).[56]

The above income generation model represents only part of the income households receive. It focuses on income generation in non-agricultural sectors and translates changes in labor incomes and the formal-informal composition of employment into poverty and distributional changes. Other income sources include income from traditional agricultural activities (including home-consumed production) and all kinds of transfer incomes from remittances to public transfers. Agricultural incomes of smallholders from the household survey will be scaled up using a weighted real factor price index for traditional agriculture (real factor

---

56 To adjust to the targets, we need to vary the constants in the occupational choice equations differently for unskilled and skilled labour, respectively. This implies that we fix the (absolute) differences between the occupational choice model constants for heads, spouses, and others for both unskilled and skilled labour. If one thinks of this problem in terms of solving the system of equations to reach the new target values, this means that the occupational constants (i.e. for heads, spouses, and others) for each skilled segment are augmented by the same amount. We now have 5 variables (2 "vectors" of constants of the choice models and 3 wage/profit constants) and 5 equations. The system is solved using a Newton-Raphson algorithm.

prices for land and unskilled labor are weighted with the share in value added of the sector). Changes in public transfers and changes in other income sources will not be taken into account in our counterfactual microsimulation of the gas boom. Public transfers will also grow or decrease in accordance with the CGE model. It should however be borne in mind that these income sources and changes therein do not affect individual behavior (at least in our model).

3.4. Results

3.4.1. Stylized simulations for link variables

While in the gas shock simulations presented below all link variables change simultaneously, the importance of specific labor market link variables for poverty and inequality can be seen more clearly if they are considered in isolation. Consequently, we performed stylized simulations for each link variable, the results of which are reported in Table 3.4. Since the mechanics of the income generation model can be better understood when looking at the urban population only, we restrict the results to this group. It turns out that, at constant factor prices, a lower formal employment share (by 5 percentage points) leads to a significant rise in urban poverty. The effect is markedly stronger for skilled workers. Yet, urban mean per capita income declines by 2.93 percent when informality increases among unskilled labor, much more strongly than the 1.76 percent decline recorded for skilled labor. This seemingly paradox result can be explained by looking at the distributional shifts. Whereas increasing informality is equalizing for unskilled labor, as indicated by the decrease in the Theil-Index, it is inequality increasing for skilled labor. This rise in inequality reinforces the negative poverty effect of declining incomes for skilled workers.

A more detailed analysis of the distributional impact that looks at the entire distribution rather than aggregate indicators reveals striking results (see App. Figure 3.2 and App. Figure 3.3): for both unskilled and skilled labor, the very poor are affected most by increasing informality. These results can be rationalized by looking at who moves into informality as well as the size of the income loss for movers relative to both their initial income and the income losses incurred by other individuals. The size of the income loss depends on individual characteristics (as the returns to these characteristics differ between formal and informal activities) and on whether an individual joins an already existing household enterprise or establishes a new one. From the estimation that underlies the microsimulation we know that less educated younger (and hence poorer) individuals tend to move into informality first. As regards the size of the income losses, the estimation results for wages and profit functions indicate that the income loss of moving into informality is higher for more educated individuals, at least in absolute terms, when they move into an existing household enterprise. Since the constant in the wage function for skilled labor is lower than the constant in the informal profit function, it may also happen that establishing an informal enterprise increases earnings for a skilled individual conditional of course on other individual characteristics. For an unskilled individual, by contrast, moving into informality will always imply an income loss, which explains the overall decrease of per capita incomes. It is the combination of these effects that explains the poverty and distributional outcomes.[57]

That overall income losses for unskilled labor are higher than for skilled labor can hence be explained by two factors. First, unskilled labor always loses when moving into informality. In addition, they are more likely to move into an existing enterprise instead of establishing a new one. For both the unskilled and skilled workforce, the move of less educated (and hence poor) individuals explains the strong negative income growth in the lower parts of the income distribution, as the incurred losses are relatively large compared to initial income. A similar reasoning explains why unskilled workers from middle-income classes do not suffer significant income losses. Fewer formal workers lose their jobs and if they do their relative income loss is not too high. Yet, higher educational endowments are associated with higher income losses, which is why the growth incidence curve is downward sloping for higher incomes. This effect seems to overcompensate the general effect that the relative importance of income losses decreases with higher incomes and explains the overall "positive" distributional impact among unskilled workers.

The negative distributional shift when informality increases among skilled workers is not only due to the strong losses of the poor. The very rich do not seem to be affected at all or even experience slightly positive income gains. This is mainly due to the very low incidence of informal work among high-skilled workers. In addition, these individuals are likely to set up a new household enterprise instead of moving into an existing one.

Table 3.4: Marginal effects of changes in link variables on urban inequality and poverty (point differences)

Scenario	P0	P1	Theil
	Urban		
Initial	50.8	23.5	63.3
5 % point decline in formal share unskilled	0.7	0.5	-1.2
5% point decline in formal share skilled	1.7	0.9	1.2
10 % increase in unskilled wages	-0.9	-0.7	-1.1
10 % increase in skilled wages	-0.7	-0.4	2.4
10 % increase in informal profits	-1.6	-1.1	-1.3

Source: Authors' calculations.

The poverty and distributional effects of increases in different types of labor incomes are in line with expectations. An increase in unskilled wages decreases poverty and improves the distribution of income. Maybe somewhat less obvious is the relatively strong reduction in the headcount index associated with an increase

---

57   Furthermore, differences in the variance of the simulated residual also play a role for the distributional impact, but this effect should not be too large.

in skilled wages. Yet, the impact on P1 is much less pronounced, indicating that the "skilled poor" are close to the poverty line, and the overall income distribution worsens quite substantially compared to the distributional improvements that can be reached e.g. by an increase in unskilled wages. Increases in informal profits turn out to reduce poverty most effectively.

3.4.2. Gas shock simulations

We now turn to a counterfactual analysis of the gas shock. We use the CGE model in combination with the microsimulation model to evaluate the distributional and poverty impacts of a gas boom over the period 1997-2005 by simulating two scenarios. The *first scenario* combines a positive temporary demand (investment) shock with a delayed positive supply shock. The size of the shocks roughly corresponds to what Bolivia actually experienced (see 3.2). The demand shock consists of a doubling of real investment demand in exploration and pipeline construction over the period 1998-2001, which is financed by foreign capital inflows. After 2001, foreign direct investment in the oil and gas sector is assumed to fall back to the pre-shock level. The upfront investment is assumed to induce a positive supply shock from 2004 onwards, which is modeled by quadrupling oil and gas reserves, i.e. the specific factor used in oil and gas production. The *second scenario* combines the first scenario with a progressive reallocation of parts of public revenues to households, as observed in the household surveys. More specifically, it is assumed that real government transfers to poor rural, poor urban, and all rich households increase by 100%, 50% and 10% (and again by 50%, 25%, and 5%), respectively, from year 2000 (from year 2004) onwards. This scenario takes into account the mainly transfer-induced rise in public deficits that occurred before the government received higher revenues from oil and gas extraction.

Benchmark: In the benchmark simulation, real GDP growth is exogenously fixed and assumed to increase by four percent annually over the period 1997-2005, while the growth rate of labor productivity is calibrated for each year so as to keep growth constant over time. This implies steadily increasing labor productivity growth over the whole simulation period. Yet, the assumption that productivity growth is only labor-augmenting is not appropriate for Bolivia. We therefore assumed a balanced growth path along which capital per worker, measured in efficiency units, remains constant over time, and calibrated the growth rate of capital productivity, which keeps the capital-labor ratio constant. At given labor growth rates and given capital accumulation rates, this implies increasing capital productivity at a decreasing rate over the total simulation period.[58]

The most striking distributional result of the benchmark simulation is the lack of significant progress with regard to poverty reduction despite relatively high

---

58 In the policy simulations discussed below, these calibrated productivity parameters arc kept constant, and the growth rate of GDP and the capital-labour ratio are allowed to vary endogenously.

growth rates of 4 percent. This is largely the result of rural-urban migration, which increases the supply of urban unskilled labor, thereby depressing wages and increasing the urban wage differential between skilled and unskilled workers (App. Table 3.3). As a result, urban inequality rises while poverty stays constant (Table 3.6). At the same time, migration reduces the supply of unskilled labor in rural areas and thereby increases wages. Together with increasing land rental rates, higher wages for rural unskilled workers raise the mixed income earned in agriculture (agricultural profits in App. Table 3.3) and slightly reduce poverty and income inequality in rural areas (Table 3.6). At the national level, both the incidence of poverty (P0) and the poverty gap (P1) hardly change over the period under consideration.

Gas Shock: Given that our CGE model does not allow for multiplier effects, it is not surprising that the foreign direct investment in gas exploration and the construction of pipelines is shown to have only a minor impact on aggregate economic activity. In the short run, the demand shock causes a steep rise in the price level, which even lowers real GDP, while over the medium run production capacity is slightly higher than in the base run.

The model can much more reliably capture the structural effects of the demand shock, which turn out to be sizeable. The investment boom induces a massive expansion of exploration, which clearly dominates the much less pronounced expansion of formal (pipeline) construction. As a result, the factors attracted into gas-related activities are predominantly formal capital and to a lesser extent skilled labor, exerting upward pressure on formal profits and skilled wages. Two secondary effects refine this picture. First, booming gas-related investment crowds out other investment goods, which are predominantly produced by heavy manufacturing as well as the formal and informal construction sectors. Since these sectors make intensive use of unskilled labor, the respective wage is driven down. The contraction of informal construction lowers the informalization of the economy. Second, the rise in the price level, which at a fixed exchange rate implies a real appreciation of about six percent in the medium run, leads to a contraction of trade-oriented sectors such as heavy manufacturing, mining, and modern agriculture, whereas sectors with low trade shares and non-traded sectors tend to expand. Among the gaining sectors with low trade-orientation, informal activities figure prominently. They realize higher returns on capital and demand additional labor, in particular unskilled workers, thus raising the informal share of unskilled labor.

As shown in Table 3.5, the investment boom is on balance associated with higher (lower) wages for skilled (unskilled) labor, higher profits in the informal urban sectors, and an increasing informalization of urban production activities, as indicated by lower formal unskilled employment shares compared to the base run. The net result of the informalization and the rise in the wage gap on the one hand, and increasing informal profits on the other, is that aggregate indicators of urban poverty and inequality hardly change (Table 3.6). In addition, lower wages for unskilled workers reduce incentives to migrate from traditional agriculture.

Nevertheless, agricultural per-capita income increases slightly as a result of higher prices for agricultural products, which in turn leads to a slight reduction of rural poverty.

In contrast to the investment demand shock, the subsequent extraction of gas from new fields significantly raises real GDP growth to almost 6 percent on average over the period 2004-2005. A rise in the aggregate price level and a significant improvement of the government budget balance through additional revenues are among the other important macroeconomic consequences of the gas shock.

The growth process induced by the gas shock is not sectorally balanced. The primary and most pronounced effect is the expansion of oil&gas and oil refining, the main downstream activity. This drives up formal capital prices and skilled wages, as these sectors are capital and skilled labor intensive. Furthermore, the reduction of the budget deficit is reflected in markedly higher investment demand by the government, which benefits both formal and informal construction. Making intensive use of unskilled labor, the construction sectors drive up unskilled wages via increased labor demand. Since the informal construction sector is particularly unskilled-labor intensive, the share of unskilled workers employed in the informal sector goes up as a result of the construction boom. As in the case of the investment shock, a real appreciation leads to a reallocation of resources from more to less trade-oriented sectors including most informal activities, which reinforces the informalization of the economy. The effect is, however, quantitatively less important than that running via investment in construction.

Increased demand for skilled labor causes the unskilled-skilled wage gap to increase. Again, this increase as well as the rising importance of lower-paid informal employment is compensated by increases in informal profits so that overall urban inequality remains largely unchanged. The significant poverty reduction appears to be entirely growth-induced. It is larger in urban areas, which directly benefit from higher gas extraction while rural areas benefit only indirectly from higher demand for agricultural products and a moderate rise in rural-urban migration. Even though the Theil index barely changes within regions, the national income distribution slightly worsens as the income gains are biased towards urban households.

Gas Shock plus Transfers: A redistribution of royalties and other revenues from the public to private households has essentially two primary effects: First, it increases disposable household income, consumption and household savings. Second, it increases current public expenditures and therefore reduces public savings. This will have secondary effects on overall income, inequality and poverty. At given household marginal propensities to consume and to save, the redistribution leads to a restructuring of final demand from investment demand towards private consumption. This is because the fall in government investment is not fully offset by a rise in private investment. Lower investment means lower capital accumulation and thus lower growth compared to the isolated gas shock scenario. The reduction of investment demand is mostly felt in the construction sector, both formal and informal, which reduces its production by 15 and 20 percent in 2001 and 2005, respectively. By the same reasoning as above, this leads to lower wages for unskilled labor and a lower informal share among unskilled workers. The latter effect is, however, offset by increased labor demand from all other informal sectors, which expand their production in response to a real appreciation caused by the expansionary government policy.

Regarding the overall changes in link variables, the redistribution policy hence appears to reinforce the results of the gas shock, with a widening wage gap, a slight increase in informal employment shares, as well as a further upturn in informal and agricultural profits. The corresponding poverty and distributional results, given in Table 3.6, only reflect the changes in labor market linkage variables. The direct effects of the transfers on disposable household income will be analyzed separately below.[59] In urban areas, both the headcount ratio and the poverty gap fall somewhat in 2001, driven by the rise in informal profits that offsets the negative effects of further increased informality and falling unskilled wages. Owing to considerably higher profits in traditional agriculture that result from increasing demand for agricultural products distributional and poverty results look more favorable for rural areas.

Table 3.5: CGE results for link variables (shocks compared to BaU)

	Agricultural profits	Informal profits	Unskilled wage	Skilled wage	Unskilled formal share	Skilled formal share
Gas shock						
2001	101.5	103.9	98.6	102.3	-0.91	-0.04
2005	103.8	108.4	105.4	109.2	-1.19	0.06
Gas shock plus transfers						
2001	107.5	104.8	97.9	103.2	-0.98	-0.15
2005	113.6	109.5	102.6	108.4	-1.40	-0.20

Source: Authors' calculations.

Note: The table shows percentage changes compared to the BaU for profits and wages. The differences in formal employment shares for unskilled and skilled labor are percentage point differences to the BaU.

---

59 The 2001 household survey, which is used in the microsimulation model, contains the Bolivida transfer payments. Simulating the "targeting" implied by the Bolivida and other public transfers goes beyond the scope of this chapter. We later illustrate the incidence of public transfers schemes by some exploratory simulations.

Table 3.6: Poverty and distributional results (point differences to BaU)

Scenario		All			Urban			Rural		
		P0	P1	Theil	P0	P1	Theil	P0	P1	Theil
Initial	1997	61.2	35.0	76.8	50.8	23.5	63.3	77.8	53.3	73.6
BaU	2001	61.3	34.7	77.6	51.2	23.5	64.6	77.4	52.5	72.6
	2005	60.8	34.1	78.2	50.8	23.2	65.4	76.7	51.5	71.8
Gas shock	2001	-0.3	-0.3	-0.1	-0.2	-0.4	-0.1	-0.3	-0.3	0.0
	2005	-2.3	-1.3	0.4	-3.0	-1.6	0.2	-1.3	-1.0	0.2
Gas shock plus	2001	-0.8	-0.8	-0.4	-0.7	-0.6	0.0	-0.8	-1.2	-1.1
transfers	2005	-2.6	-1.9	-0.6	-3.2	-1.6	0.0	-1.7	-2.4	-1.6

Source: Authors' calculations.

To investigate the possible primary poverty and distributional impact of transfers, we conducted a stylized microsimulation in which we raised the transfers as observed in the household survey (PAYG pensions, Bonosol payments, and other social transfers) by 10 percent. If all households were covered by the transfer scheme, per capita incomes increase by one percent, which can also be interpreted as the cost of increasing the transfers (Table 3.7). Strikingly, while P0 indicates some transfer-induced poverty reduction, P1 does not. This can easily be explained when looking at the growth incidence curve given in App. Figure 3.4, which points to a very bad targeting, where the poorest 50 percent of the population benefit less than proportionately. The shape of the growth incidence curve also illustrates that aggregate indicators of inequality, such as the Theil index that barely changes in this experiment, may well be misleading.

Table 3.7: Poverty and distributional impact of increases in public transfers

Scenario	P0	P1	Theil	Resource cost
	National			
Initial	61.2	35.0	76.8	
10 % increase in public transfers	-0.7	-0.1	-0.1	0.97

Source: Authors' calculations.

Note: The resource cost refers to the increase in per capita income implied by the transfer.

3.5. Concluding remarks

In this chapter, we combined a computable general equilibrium model with a microsimulation model to analyze numerically the short to medium-run impact of Bolivia's booming gas sector on poverty and income distribution. This approach accounts for major transmission mechanisms through which the gas boom affects the distribution of income. It captures microeconomic determinants of distributional such as the occupational choices between formal and informal employment and the corresponding changes in earnings at the individual level, as well as macroeconomic and sectoral determinants such as relative factor prices, rural-urban migration and informalization of production and employment. By focusing on poverty and distributional effects and by distinguishing informal and formal activities, our analysis adds a new perspective to the existing literature, which largely consists of macroeconomic studies based on the dichotomy between tradable and non-tradable sectors.

Our simulation results suggest that the gas boom and the expansion of public transfers have both unequalizing and equalizing distributional impacts that tend to offset each other. As net distributional change is limited, growth generated by the boom also reduces poverty and the boom hence does not completely bypass the poorer parts of the Bolivian population. Poverty reduction with little distributional change can be observed despite increasing informality. Using stylized microsimulation experiments, we illustrate that lower formal employment can lead to a significant rise in urban poverty and that the very poor are affected most by increasing informality. Yet, considerable overall increases in informal profits compensate this possible negative impact. Informalization and increasing informal profits during the investment boom mainly result from contractions of investment good and trade-oriented sectors (cost-push). When gas exports pick up, demand for informally produced non-tradables increases (demand-pull) and formal sectors are hurt by real appreciation. The positive distributional impact of increased informal profits also masks the inequality-increasing impact of the widening of the unskilled-skilled wage gap that is particularly strong during the initial investment boom. Regarding the increase in public transfers, the government's redistribution policy is largely ineffective in reducing poverty as it is poorly targeted. The indirect effects of increased public transfers tend to reinforce the informalization process and hence the distributional and poverty impacts of the gas boom. In addition, the resulting lower investment leads to lower overall economic growth.

If the increases in informal profits compensate the potentially negative poverty effects of increased informality – why should we worry about the resource-boom induced structural change? Before we shortly discuss this crucial question, we should stress that this chapter examines the reallocation processes induced by a gas boom and their distributional consequences in a time horizon of approximately one decade. Yet, only in a longer time horizon, sectoral externalities might come into effect, which render this reallocation towards informal activities worrisome. We think there are good reasons to believe that a sectoral pattern of change characterized by specialization into certain non-tradables and informalization can permanently damage a country's development prospects, although concrete empirical evidence is scarce. Manufacturing sectors that contract considerably in the Bolivian case are widely viewed as exhibiting important learning by doing effects. In addition, informal sectors may exhibit important negative externalities, as employment is often unstable and employees are typically not covered by any kind of social insurance. Such precarious employment is likely to have negative effects on human capital accumulation. If this pessimism about the sectoral change is valid, Bolivia's natural gas abundance may be seen as a curse rather than a blessing.[60] However, the relationship between resource abundance and low economic growth and little poverty reduction is not a law; rather, it presents a challenge to find appropriate policies to avoid the pitfalls. While designing a coherent strategy towards this end is extremely difficult, redistribution of resource rents could make a dent in poverty – if targeted effectively.

---

60 Sachs and Warner (1997) note with regard to larger positive externalities in manufacturing that this assumption "remains somewhat speculative". This assessment still holds today and also applies to possible negative externalities of informal employment. In light of increasing informalization in many Latin American economies the latter may constitute an interesting area for future research.

3.6. Appendices

3.6.1. Additional figures

App. Figure 3.1: The construction sector, 1995 = 100

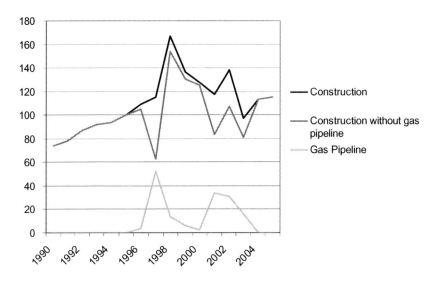

Source: INE (www.ine.gov.bo, 2005).

App. Figure 3.2: Growth incidence curve, 5 point decline in formal employment for unskilled labor

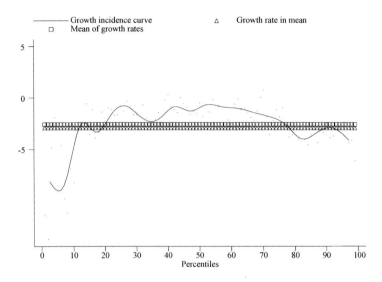

Source: Authors' calculations.

*App. Figure 3.3: Growth incidence curve, 5 point decline in formal employment
         for skilled labor*

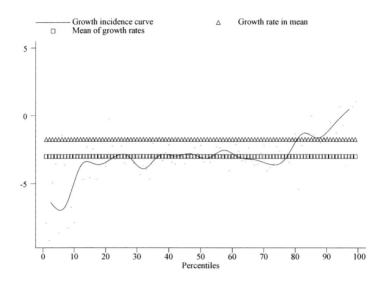

Source: Authors' calculations.

App. Figure 3.4: Growth incidence curve, 10 percent increase in transfers to all households

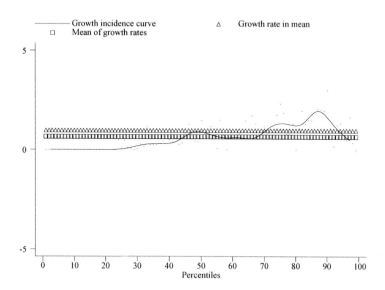

Source: Authors' calculations.

3.6.2. Additional tables

App. Table 3.1: Estimation results for the logit choice models, choices are dichotomous variables with formal = 1, informal = 1

Explanatory var	dep var		
	Head's choice	Spouse's choice	Other's choice
Education	-0.19	-0.323	-0.219
	(5.30)**	(5.19)**	(3.17)**
Education squared	0.018	0.026	0.023
	(9.30)**	(7.85)**	(6.06)**
Experience	-0.012	-0.011	0.005
	(3.81)**	-1.36	-0.57
Female dummy	-1.089	-0.857	-0.756
	(11.16)**	(2.70)**	(3.44)**
Formal employment share in province	4.624	3.24	4.008
	(10.38)**	(3.70)**	(4.51)**
Indigenous dummy		-0.629	
		(3.07)**	
Beni dummy		0.486	
		-1.75	
Pando dummy		0.734	
		(2.03)*	
No of children under 10		0.448	0.107
		(2.53)*	-1.49
Interaction female*no of children		-0.391	-0.221
		(2.06)*	(2.07)*
Head's formal sector wage		0.193	0.131
		(8.05)**	(5.51)**
Widow dummy		0.579	
		-1.07	
Constant	-1.633	-1.686	-2.929
	(5.45)**	(2.75)**	(5.03)**
Observations	3385	1140	1102
Pseudo R2	0.1716	0.2693	0.1943

Robust z statistics in parentheses
* significant at 5%; ** significant at 1%

Source: Authors' calculations.

App. Table 3.2: Estimation results for the wage and profit equations

Explanatory var	Formal unskilled wages	dep var Formal skilled wages	Informal profits
Education	0.084 (9.16)**	0.152 (13.53)**	
Experience	0.051 (11.20)**	0.057 (7.96)**	
Experience squared	-0.001 (9.54)**	-0.001 (4.72)**	
Female dummy	-0.627 (11.37)**	-0.373 (8.71)**	
Potosi dummy	-0.182 (2.18)*	-0.17 -1.78	-0.452 (3.34)**
Tarija dummy	0.307 (3.62)**	0.15 -1.59	0.137 -1.34
Santa Cruz	0.193 (2.77)**	0.246 (3.63)**	0.065 -1.01
Beni dummy	0.374 (4.81)**	0.175 (2.30)*	0.171 -1.73
Pando dummy	0 0	0.258 (2.49)*	0.792 (4.30)**
Avg. education			0.059 (8.64)**
Avg. experience			0.038 (8.44)**
Avg. experience squared			-0.001 (8.20)**
Number of females			-0.602 (13.87)**
Number of enterprise			1.332 (20.07)**
Constant	5.092 (45.57)**	4.258 (25.40)**	4.947 (48.74)**
Observations	1357	1407	1905
R-squared	0.26	0.27	0.31

Robust t statistics in parentheses
* significant at 5%; ** significant at 1%

Source: Authors' calculations.

App. Table 3.3: Business as Usual (BaU) scenario

Variable	1997	2001	2005
GDP growth rate		4.00	4.00
Price level	1.00	0.97	0.94
Growth rate of capital productivity		1.45	1.15
Growth rate of labor productivity		1.56	1.61
Labor demand			
Skilled labor	1.00	1.11	1.23
Rural unskilled labor	1.00	1.06	1.13
Urban unskilled labor	1.00	1.16	1.34
Migration	1.00	0.87	0.78
Capital demand			
Formal capital	1.00	1.11	1.25
Informal capital	1.00	1.12	1.27
Link variables			
Agricultural profits	1.00	1.06	1.13
Informal profits	1.00	1.00	1.00
Unskilled wage	1.00	0.97	0.97
Skilled wage	1.00	1.03	1.07
Formal share unskilled	0.38	0.38	0.39
Formal share skilled	0.72	0.71	0.71

Source: Authors' calculations.

4. Structural change and poverty reduction in Brazil: The impact of the Doha Round

4.1. Introduction

Trade liberalization, in particular the liberalization of trade in agricultural products, is considered by many observers as one of the key components of a strategy to reduce poverty worldwide. In their review of the relationship between trade liberalization and poverty, Winters, McCulloch and McKay (2004), conclude that trade liberalization "may be one of the most cost-effective anti-poverty policies available to governments" although it may not be the most powerful. Yet, the complex relationship between trade, growth, distribution and poverty does not allow for a simple conclusion with regard to the impact of trade liberalization on poverty, as the poverty outcomes of trade liberalization may vary substantially from case to case. Despite the complexity of this relationship the evidence so far provides enough insights to predict at least the largest impacts (Winters, McCulloch, and McKay 2004). One of these insights is the importance of the impact of trade liberalization on wages and employment, which depends on the structure and the functioning of the labor market.

For the Brazilian case, this chapter intends to evaluate the poverty effects of trade liberalization in the medium run. In doing so, we focus on the labor market, as we consider this transmission channel to be of overriding importance in this time horizon. This implies to assess the poverty impact of a Doha Round (and a Full Liberalization)[61] counterfactual scenario against a scenario that incorporates some of the main features of medium run structural change. We will thus examine whether the effects of trade liberalization, in particular on poverty and the distribution of income, are still prominent in the medium run.

Recent research has demonstrated that growth can differ tremendously in its power to reduce poverty both across countries and over time.[62] In particular, in high-inequality countries such as Brazil, an apparently slight worsening of the income distribution can imply that growth has very little impact on poverty. It is hence not only important by how much trade liberalization raises incomes, but how it affects the pattern of income growth. The driving forces of this pattern work through the labor market. Among them are changes in relative factor prices, but also changes in endowments play an important role in the medium run, as for

---

61 The global trade liberalization scenarios will not be discussed in this chapter. The trade shocks that the Brazilian economy faces were developed by a team examining the economic effects of likely Doha negotiation outcomes using a (GTAP-based) global trade model. We will comment only on the changes in tariffs and international prices, as they affect the Brazilian economy. Detailed information on the scenarios and the global trade model used to investigate their economic effects are available from the authors on request, as the project output has not been published yet.

62 See Ravallion (2001a), Ravallion and Datt (1999), World Bank (2005b), Grimm, Klasen, and McKay (2006) or Kappel, Lay and Steiner (2005).

example the workforce advances its skills. In addition, sectoral employment change can contribute significantly to poverty reduction. Such change in the structure of employment can have very large effects on poverty, as it may enable people to escape poverty traps. There is quite some evidence on the existence of such poverty traps that can arise if occupational or technology choices are discrete and there exist fixed or sunk costs to choosing a higher return occupation or technology (Barrett 2004). Moving out of agriculture where poverty rates are often much higher than in other sectors is one example for such choices. This latter issue is of particular interest in the Brazilian context, as there has been a massive reduction in agricultural employment in recent years, which we consider to be likely to continue. This reduction in agricultural employment may have contributed to poverty reduction, as poverty among agricultural households is considerably higher than among non-agricultural households. Trade liberalization that one would expect to favor agriculture in Brazil may thus work against the "natural" forces of structural change with an adverse impact on poverty reduction. However, trade liberalization may also relieve some of the pressure put on non-agricultural incomes by the reduction in agricultural employment and have some direct poverty reducing effect through raising agricultural incomes.

This last example illustrates the necessity of quantifying each of these transmission channels to evaluate the overall poverty and distributional impact of trade reform. The features incorporated in our simulation exercise are therefore changes in different sources of factor income, changes in the sectoral composition of the workforce, and educational upgrading of the workforce. These changes are driven by changing consumption patterns, purely exogenous factors (at least in our model), such as differentials in productivity growth rates across sectors and differential growth rates for different types of labor, and, finally, the trade shocks. The methodology used here combines a dynamic computable general equilibrium model with a microsimulation model for Brazil. For a time horizon of 15 years, a business as usual scenario and two trade counterfactuals are developed in the CGE model and crucial aggregate results on relative factor prices and resource movements from agricultural to non-agricultural sectors are linked to a microsimulation. This macro-micro model enables us to analyze the long-term poverty and distributional impact of different growth patterns.

The chapter is structured as follows. We first provide some background information on the Brazilian case and motivate our approach. Then, we describe the macro and micro modules of the model. The results of our simulations are reported and commented in the following section. The last section summarizes and concludes.

4.2. Background and motivation

The main objective of this chapter is to assess whether trade reform favors the Brazilian poor. It is therefore important to know who the poor are, where they live, and especially how they earn their living. In addition, it should prove helpful to identify economic trends that have been particularly important for the poor.

Brazil's per capita income has virtually stagnated for the past 25 years and the very unequal distribution of income has remained more or less unchanged. Accordingly, poverty in Brazil has been roughly constant over the past 25 years (Bourguignon, Ferreira, and Lustig 2005b; Verner 2004). In light of the substantial structural changes that have occurred in this period, especially increasing urbanization, a massive decline in agricultural employment, increasing unemployment, an important educational expansion and demographic changes, this appears "paradoxical", as Bourguignon et al. (2005b) put it. Yet, micro-imulation exercises by Ferreira and Paes de Barros (2005) show that each of the features of structural change affects poverty and inequality, but they tend to cancel out each other.[63]

Poverty in Brazil varies considerably between regions, rural and urban areas, and city sizes with poverty being particularly high in rural areas, small and medium towns and the metropolitan peripheries of the North and the Northeast (Ferreira, Lanjouw, and Neri 2001). In 1996, the North and the Northeast accounted for 55 percent of the poor and for 34 percent of the Brazilian population. At the national level, about 20 percent of the population lived in rural areas contributing 35 percent to total poverty.[64] The high poverty rates in rural areas, particularly in the Northeast, are related to this region's predominance of employment in agriculture. The Northeast has the highest share of agriculture in employment with 34 percent in 2001 compared to only 11.5 percent in the Southeast.[65] According to Ferreira, Lanjouw, and Neri (2001), 20 percent of all households had a household head employed in agriculture and these households contributed 34 percent to overall poverty in 1996.

Yet, not only do poverty levels differ across regions, rural and urban areas, and activities, but also do the changes in poverty. Verner's (2004) PNAD-based[66] figures suggest that the poverty headcount in the Northeast declined from almost 60 percent in 1990 to 42.3 percent in 2001, whereas poverty in Brazil's most populous state Sao Paulo rose slightly from 8.6 to 9.4 percent during the same period. For urban areas, Ferreira and Paes de Barros (2005) show that extreme poverty increased between 1976 and 1996. According to Paes de Barros (2004) however, the poverty incidence in rural areas in general and among households engaged in agricultural activities, in particular, declined from levels of about 60 percent to around 50 percent between 1992 and 2001.

One important factor for understanding these developments are the structural changes in Brazilian agriculture in the 1980s and 1990s. These changes have

---

63 Note that their analysis compares the income distribution of 1976 with the 1996 distribution. For detailed results see Ferreira and Paes de Barros (2005).

64 Poverty is measured by the headcount ratio. The poverty figures in this paragraph are taken from Ferreira, Lanjouw, and Neri (2001).

65 The figures on agricultural employment are own calculations based on the PNAD 1997 and the PNAD 2001.

66 The PNAD (Pesquisa Nacional por Amostra de Domicílios) is a regularly conducted representative household survey.

certainly had a profound impact on rural livelihoods and poverty in Brazil, but they may also have affected urban areas for example by putting pressure on urban labor markets through increased migration. With the exception of Paes de Barros (2004), research efforts in this direction however have focused on agricultural performance rather than on how this performance affects people's livelihoods. In their assessment of the impact of sector-specific as well as economy-wide reforms on Brazilian agriculture, Helfand and Rezende (2004) conclude that agriculture became one of the most dynamic sectors in the Brazilian economy. Between 1980 and 1998 real GDP grew by about 40 percent and real agricultural output by about 70 percent. In many sub-sectors, yields increased significantly and more harvested area was dedicated to exportables, in particular soybeans and sugarcane. Agriculture benefited from a conducive macroeconomic environment and trade reforms that led to less industrial protection and the elimination of taxes and quantitative restrictions on agricultural exports. In addition, specific agricultural reforms – in particular a reform of agricultural credit and price support policies; an agrarian reform program, including a land reform; and, finally, the deregulation of domestic markets for agricultural goods – were important drivers of the observed agricultural performance.[67] The increase in agricultural productivity however was accompanied by a massive lay-off of hired labor and by important changes in the size distribution of farms. According to the agricultural census from 1996, the number of small farms declined dramatically and agricultural employment shrank by 23 percent between 1986 and 1996, although these figures should be taken with caution (Helfand and Rezende 2004). Non-agricultural activities appear to have compensated for the loss in agricultural employment in rural areas, but unemployment rates in urban areas with a previously important share of agricultural labor have risen in that period (Dias and Amaral 2002). Our analysis based on the 1997 and 2001 household surveys (PNAD) suggests that this decline in agricultural employment has continued after 1996. In 2001, agriculture accounted for 20.6 percent of employment in Brazil down from 24.2 percent in 1997. Unemployment in rural areas has stayed constant at about 2.5 percent during this period, whereas urban unemployment has risen from 9.44 to 10.6 percent, an increase that may be related to the decline in agricultural employment.[68] Less agricultural employment opportunities may also be one of the reasons for further urbanization in Brazil although it is difficult to establish this link empirically, as we explain in more detail later. The rural population declined quite dramatically from 24.41 percent in 1991 to 21.64 percent in 1996 (IBGE 1997) and 16 percent in 2001 (PNAD 2001, authors' own calculations). The trends in rural poverty

---

67 See Helfand and Rezende (2004) and Dias and Amaral (2002) for details.

68 Data from employment histories in the PNAD reveal that in both 1997 and 2001 about 6 percent of those who became unemployed in the last year were employed in agricultural sectors before. Taking into account that approx. 20 percent of the workforce are employed in agriculture, this figure is rather low and may be taken as a sign that the rise in urban unemployment is not causally linked to the decline in agricultural employment.

mentioned above suggest that the described developments have improved rural livelihoods. Nevertheless, poverty rates in rural areas remain well above urban poverty rates.

Future developments in agriculture are not known with certainty, but it is likely that some of the observed trends, in particular the decline in agricultural employment and the related, though very small, increase in incomes from agriculture, will continue. We therefore incorporate them in our Business as Usual (BaU) scenario, against which the trade reform scenarios are to be judged. The BaU scenario should hence provide a quantitative assessment of the poverty and income distribution effects of these possible future developments. Trade liberalization may have important consequences in this regard through potentially favoring export-oriented agricultural sectors, possibly offsetting at least some of the decrease in agricultural employment, and increasing agricultural incomes.

So far, we have been mainly concerned with the rural poor and the developments in the agricultural sector. More than two thirds of the Brazilian poor however either live in urban areas or from income earned in non-agricultural sectors. They may have been only indirectly affected by the intersectoral resource shifts just described, for example through downward pressure on non-agricultural wages because of labor released from agriculture. Ferreira and Paes de Barros (2005) find the abovementioned increase in extreme poverty in urban Brazil to be related to rising unemployment and informality. In addition, lower labor market returns contributed to higher poverty. These negative effects on poverty were partially offset by demographic developments, but mainly by educational expansion. In this regard, it should also be noted that low levels of education are an important determinant of poverty in Brazil. Educational expansion has hence become a major policy focus of the Brazilian government for good reasons.[69] Better education, in particular for the poor, is of course only one of the many factors that decide upon whether and how the poor benefit from growth. Social conflict and crime, deficient public service delivery as well as unemployment, in particular youth unemployment and a high share of informal work relations and self-employment are pressing problems in the metropolitan areas and their peripheries. Some of the latter issues certainly go beyond the scope of our analysis, but the decline of the informal sector as well as urban unemployment are key factors for poverty reduction. The poverty incidence among informal sector employees and the urban self-employed is almost as high as among rural self-employed (Elbers, Lanjouw, Lanjouw and Leite 2004).

Unfortunately, it is very difficult to empirically model the informal economy and formal-informal linkages without making very crude assumptions, for example on informal technologies, which is why we decided not to model informal

---

69 The Bolsa Escola Program, a means-tested conditional cash transfer program that reaches 6 million households in Brazil, is one of the major policy instruments in this regard. See Bourguignon, Ferreira and Leite (2002) for an assessment of Bolsa Escola using a microsimulation model.

activities explicitly. With regard to trade liberalization, it may of course well be that informal and formal activities are affected differently by trade reform, due to differences in technologies as well as export-orientation. Furthermore, our model is a full-employment model and we hence disregard unemployment, which may also arise, at least transitorily, due to trade liberalization. Admittedly, our poverty impact analysis may therefore miss some of the transmission channels through which trade liberalization affects especially the urban poor. We do however make an attempt to represent further educational expansion in our simulations.

All in all, our analysis hence addresses the poverty and distributional impact of a subset of features of structural change that we consider particularly relevant for the Brazilian case (and possibly beyond Brazil), most importantly further structural change in agriculture, and how these features interact with trade policies.

4.3.   The modeling framework

The model consists of a sequentially dynamic CGE model that is linked to a microimulation. The microsimulation takes the changes in factor and goods prices as given; hence, there is no feedback between these two parts of the model. We consider this framework particularly suited for the questions at hand, as the CGE model captures some of the main features of structural change and the relative price changes accompanying them. The microsimulation then allows for a detailed empirical assessment of the household responses to these changes. As will become clear in the following, the major advantage of the microsimulation is that its micro unit is the individual rather than the household, which offers much richer ways of representing distributional dynamics.

4.3.1. The macro model

A 1997 Social Accounting Matrix (SAM) has been used as the initial benchmark equilibrium for the CGE model. This SAM has been assembled from various sources incorporating data from the 1997 Input Output table, information from the SAM assembled by Harrison, Rutherford, Tarr, and Gurgel (2003), and the 2001 PNAD household survey. For the purposes of this model the full SAM – which includes 41 sectors, 41 commodities, 12 factors (skilled and unskilled labor by gender and by farm and non-farm occupation, agricultural and non-agricultural capital, land and natural resources), an aggregate household account, and other accounts (government, savings and investment, and rest of the world)[70] – has been aggregated to a smaller size and it comprises the accounts shown in Table 4.1.

---

70   See annex for a full list of accounts.

Table 4.1: CGE Model accounts

Model Sectors

1	CerealGrains	7	OilMinerals	13	MachineryEquipment
2	OilSeeds	8	LightManufacturing	14	OtherServices
3	RawSugar	9	AgriIndustriesExp	15	Construction
4	OthCrops	10	WoodProductsPaper	16	TradeCommunication
5	Livestock	11	ChemicalsOilPr	17	PublicServices
6	RawAnimalProducts	12	MetalMineralProducts		

Factors of Production

18	Land	21	Non-Agriculture Unskil. Lab	23	Agriculture Unskil. Lab
19	Natural Resources	22	Non-Agriculture Skilled Lab	24	Agriculture Skilled Lab
20	Capital				

Other Accounts

25	Production Taxes	29	Direct Taxes	32	Investment-Savings
26	Indirect Taxes	30	Households	33	Variation of Stocks
27	Tariffs	31	Government	34	Rest of the World
28	Export Taxes				

The CGE model is based on a standard neoclassical dynamic general equilibrium model and the following subsections describe its main features. Given our focus on labor markets and dynamic structural trends, more detailed explanations are provided on the modeling of factor markets and growth.

Production. Output results from nested CES (Constant Elasticity of Substitution) functions that, at the top level, combine intermediate and value added aggregates. At the second level, on the one hand, the intermediate aggregate is obtained combining all products in fixed proportions (Leontief structure), and, on the other hand, value added results by aggregating the primary factors. At this level, primary factors are a capital-labor bundle and aggregate land. Lower levels disaggregate capital and labor, and then labor into different categories.

Income Distribution and Absorption. Labor income and capital revenues are allocated to households according to a fixed coefficient distribution matrix derived from the original SAM. Notice that one of the main advantages of using the micro-module is to enrich, as described above, this rather crude macro distribution mechanism. Private consumption demand is obtained through maximization of household specific utility function following the Linear Expenditure System (LES). Private savings are a fixed proportion of income. Once the total value of private consumption is determined, government and investment demands[71] are disaggregated in sectoral demands according to fixed coefficient functions.

International Trade. The model assumes imperfect substitution among goods originating in different geographical areas.[72] Imports demand results from a CES aggregation function of domestic and imported goods. Export supply is

---

71 Aggregate investment is set equal to aggregate savings, while aggregate government expenditures are exogenously fixed.
72 See Armington (1969) for details.

symmetrically modeled as a Constant Elasticity of Transformation (CET) function. Producers decide to allocate their output to domestic or foreign markets responding to relative prices. The assumptions of imperfect substitution and imperfect transformability grant a certain degree of autonomy of domestic prices with respect to foreign prices and prevent the model from generating corner solutions. This single country Brazilian model has been linked to a global CGE model by adding export demand functions so that the increased market access accompanying multilateral trade liberalization scenarios can be simulated more precisely. In particular, export demands have been implemented as shown in equation (1) and, during a trade policy simulation, to mimic the quantity and price shocks resulting from the global model, both the intercept α^e_k and the price level $WPEindex$ are changed accordingly.

$$ ED_k = \alpha^e_k \left(\frac{\overline{WPEindex_k}}{WPE_k} \right)^{\eta^e_k} \tag{1} $$

No international import supply functions have been added and Brazil is a price taker for its imports. The balance of payments equilibrium is determined by the equality of foreign savings (which are exogenous) to the value for the current account.

Factor Markets. Labor is distinguished into 2 categories: skilled and unskilled. These categories are considered imperfectly substitutable inputs in the production process; moreover, some degree of market segmentation is assumed: capital and land are perfectly mobile across sectors, and natural resources are sector specific, and labor markets for the unskilled are segmented between agriculture and non-agriculture, whereas skilled workers are fully mobile.

The labor market specification is a key element of our model and an important driver of poverty and distributional results. Therefore, its specification calls for some clarification and justification. Before we enter a discussion on the specific assumptions of our model, we shortly define labor market segmentation, as the applied modeling literature often handles this term rather sloppy.[73] A common misunderstanding is that a labor market is segmented if one can identify "segments" with different wage-setting mechanisms, for example due to efficiency wages being paid to some segment of the workforce. Yet, different wage-setting causes wage rigidity that implies (price) rationing, but not segmentation. Such rationing due to different wage-setting may well be observed in an efficient, smoothly functioning labor market.[74] A segmented labor market however does not

---

73 See Taubman and Wachter (1986) for a general discussion of labor market
    segmentation.
74 Note that rationing might of course well be inefficient if is for example due to
    government interventions.

work smoothly, as labor market mobility is limited and this puts constraints on the adjustment of the supply side. Such constraints could for example be deficiencies in educational systems that prevent unskilled workers from acquiring more skills despite an increasing wage gap between unskilled and skilled labor.

As mentioned above, we assume that the labor market is segmented into unskilled and skilled labor. We think that this has become a standard assumption in CGE modeling for good reasons. The inequalities of the Brazilian society also in terms of educational endowments and more importantly, access to education and on-the-job training, certainly justify this assumption even over medium-term time horizons.

In addition, we assume that the market for unskilled labor is further segmented into agricultural and non-agricultural activities. This is without doubt a more controversial assumption, in particular in light of its importance in terms of poverty and distributional results. An obvious first check of this assumption is whether incomes in agriculture are really lower in agriculture once we control for all the "usual suspects" of wage determination, including education, experience, gender, racial dummies, other than sectoral employment-related variables, such as self-employment, being employed in the informal sector, or working only seasonally, and geographical variables that capture differences between the Brazilian regions as well as between rural and urban areas. Note that these geographical variables also capture spatial price differentials. Taking the largest non-agricultural sector in terms of employment, "other services", as a reference group, an OLS regression shows that individual labor incomes are significantly lower in all agricultural sectors except the oil seeds and the sugar cane sector, which only account for approximately 6 percent of agricultural employment. The regression results are reported in App. Table 4.4. Note that labor incomes in all non-agricultural sectors, with the notable exception of agricultural processing, are significantly higher than in "other services".[75]

There can be a number of reasons for observing this income gap between agricultural and non-agricultural employment. A first explanation could be that agricultural income, in particular from self-employment, is systematically underreported. Yet, the regression results suggest that there is no underreporting problem for the self-employed, as for example both the dummy for self-employment and the dummy for being a landowner[76] turn out to be significantly positive. It can be argued at this point that these dummies reflect the returns to land, and underreporting may still be present. Even if so, we also do not see a reason why there should be systematically more underreporting among the wage-employed in agricultural than among those in non-agricultural sectors.

---

75 Note that these equations were estimated on monthly wages, which may introduce some seasonality bias. We also do not control for hours worked. We admit that the procedure to test for segmentation is somewhat rudimentary, but besides its shortcomings it should provide a rough approximation of sectoral wage differences.

76 More than 60 percent of the agricultural self-employed work on their own land.

Another reason for the sectoral income differential may lie in positive externalities associated to agricultural employment. Examples of such externalities include food self-sufficiency or employment opportunities for other family members. Yet, you can also easily think of negative externalities of agricultural employment, such as the exposure to weather shocks or hard physical work. These externalities are difficult if not impossible to quantify and we implicitly assume that positive and negative externalities tend to cancel each other out.

If we accept that there is an income differential between agriculture and non-agricultural sectors, the question is why individuals do not respond to this differential and move to the non-agricultural sector until incomes in both sectors are equalized. There must hence be barriers to mobility between agricultural and non-agricultural employment that prevent people from moving out of the agricultural sector. When thinking about limited mobility and the reasons behind it, the time horizon of the analysis is an important issue. It should be borne in mind that the time span considered here is approximately 15 years. A very important factor also in the medium run is that many people in the agricultural sector own land. Smallholders who own their own land and non-remunerated family members on these farms account for approximately 40 percent of agricultural employment in Brazil. There may be important externalities related to land ownership, such as economic independency. Some smallholders may not sell the land they own because of a bequest motive. The specificity of human capital acquired in the agricultural sector may also play an important role in making people stay in the agricultural sector. In addition, risk aversion may also prevent people from switching from agricultural to non-agricultural activities since they will only on average gain more in non-agricultural sectors. The estimations for our microsimulation model that we comment in more detail later lend empirical support to some of these hypotheses. In particular, we find that land ownership prevents individuals from moving out of the agricultural sector.

The implementation of dual labor markets for *unskilled* workers follows the standard Harris-Todaro specification where the decision to migrate is a function of the expected income in the non agricultural (urban, in the original formulation) segment relative to the expected income in the agricultural (rural) segment. The specification deviates somewhat from Harris-Todaro. First, relative wages are used as a proxy for relative incomes. Second, actual wages determines migration rather than expected wages in the absence of unemployment. The basic migration equation has the form given in equation (2), where $MIGR$ represents the level of migration between segments. Note that the index l indicates the skill level ($l =$ unskilled), and the index g represent the segment ($g =$ agriculture or non-agriculture).

$$MIGR_l = \chi_l^m \left[\left(\frac{AWAGE_{Nagri,l}}{AWAGE_{Agri,l}} \right)^{\omega_l^m} - 1 \right] \tag{2}$$

$$AWAGE_{g,l} = \frac{\sum_{i \in g} \left(\frac{W_{i,l}}{1 + \tau_{i,l}^{fl}} \right) L_{i,l}^d}{\sum_{i \in g} L_{i,l}^d} \tag{3}$$

The variable $AWAGE$ is the average wage in the respective segments and is given by equation (3). The average wage is calculated based on the net-of-tax wage rate, the rate which matters to the worker deciding to migrate or not.

Labor market equilibrium conditions are based on two separate labor markets rather than the integrated market of the skilled workers. Equation (4) determines the equilibrium wage rate by segment—i.e. agriculture and non-agriculture. It sets the aggregate segment labor supply equal to the demand for labor in the same segment, i.e. it determines the variable W^e which is now indexed by both segment index as well as labor type. The model allows for inter-sectoral wage differentials, but these are exogenous in the standard model. Equation (5) evaluates the relative wages with respect to the segment-specific equilibrium wage.

$$L_{g,l}^s = \sum_{i \in g} L_{i,l}^d \tag{4}$$

$$W_{i,l} = \phi_{i,l}^l W_{g,l}^e \quad \text{for} \quad i \in g \tag{5}$$

The remaining loose end is the definition of labor supply and this is given by equations (6) and (7). It is assumed that labor supply net of migration is given in any given period. In the dynamic scenario, labor supply in each segment grows at the same exogenous rate, g^L and migration is subtracted from this amount in the agricultural segment, equation (6), and is added to labor supply in the non-agricultural segment, equation (7). Equation (8) determines the total economy-wide labor supply for each labor type.

$$L_{Agri,l}^s = \left(1 + g_l^L\right) L_{Agri,l,-1}^s - MIGR_l \tag{6}$$

$$L_{Nagri,l}^s = \left(1 + g_l^L\right) L_{Nagri,l,-1}^s + MIGR_l \tag{7}$$

$$L_{Tot,l}^s = L_{Agri,l}^s + L_{Nagri,l}^s \tag{8}$$

Model Closures. The equilibrium condition on the balance of payments is combined with other closure conditions so that the model can be solved for each period. Firstly consider the government budget. Its surplus is fixed and the household income tax schedule shifts in order to achieve the predetermined net government position. Secondly, investment must equal savings, which originate from households, corporations, government and rest of the world. Aggregate investment is set equal to aggregate savings, while aggregate government expenditures are exogenously fixed.

Growth equations. Sectoral shifts among agriculture and non-agriculture and human capital upgrading are two of the main features that have characterized recent growth processes in Brazil, and indeed in most developing nations. To capture these features in a transparent and simple dynamic framework, productivity growth calibration is different for the agriculture and non-agriculture sectors. Equation (9) defines the growth rate of GDP at market price and equation (10) is a formula expressing a balanced growth, where capital to labor ratio in efficiency units is constant.

$$RGDPMP = (1 + g^y) \, RGDPMP_{-1} \tag{9}$$

$$\frac{\sum_{kt}\sum_{i} \lambda^k_{i,kt} K^d_{i,kt}}{\sum_{l}\sum_{i} \lambda^l_{i,l} L^d_{i,l}} = \frac{\sum_{kt}\sum_{i} \lambda^k_{i,kt,0} K^d_{i,kt,0}}{\sum_{l}\sum_{i} \lambda^l_{i,l,0} L^d_{i,l,0}} = \chi^{kl} \tag{10}$$

Equation (11) and (12) determine the growth rates of labor and capital productivity for the non-agricultural sectors (subscript *nag*). The growth rates have two components, a uniform factor applied in all sectors to all types of labor and capital, γ^l and γ^k, and a sector- and factor-specific factor, χ^l and χ^k. In defining a baseline, the growth rate of GDP is exogenous, as well as the capital to labor ratio. In this case, equation (9) is used to calibrate the γ^l parameter and equation (10) calculates the common growth rate for capital productivity, γ^k. In policy simulations, γ^l and γ^k are given, and equation (9) defines the growth rate of GDP, whereas equation (10) estimates the capital output ratio.

$$\lambda^l_{nag,l} = (1 + \gamma^l + \chi^l_{nag,l}) \, \lambda^l_{nag,l,-1} \tag{11}$$

$$\lambda^k_{nag,kt} = (1 + \gamma^k + \chi^k_{nag,kt}) \lambda^k_{nag,kt,-1} \tag{12}$$

Productivity growth in agriculture is treated differently. As already mentioned, in the last decade, Brazilian agriculture recorded high productivity growth, and we impose exogenous growth rate for productivity in agriculture uniformly across all factors, as shown in the following equations. Equation (13) represents the increase in labor productivity in agricultural sectors not subject to the uniform productivity shift factor γ^l. Equations (14) through (16) update productivity of capital, land and the sector specific factor, respectively. With agricultural productivity assumed to be uniform across all factors of production, the growth parameters χ^l, χ^k, χ^t, χ^y will be the same for all agricultural sectors.

$$\lambda_{ag,l}^l = (1 + \chi_{ag,l}^l)\lambda_{ag,l,-1}^l \tag{13}$$

$$\lambda_{ag,kt}^k = (1 + \chi_{ag,kt}^k)\lambda_{ag,kt,-1}^k \tag{14}$$

$$\lambda_{ag,lt}^t = (1 + \chi_{ag,lt}^t)\lambda_{ag,lt,-1}^t \tag{15}$$

$$\lambda_{ag}^\gamma = (1 + \chi_{ag}^\gamma)\lambda_{ag,-1}^\gamma \tag{16}$$

Additional support for a sector specific treatment of productivity where agriculture shows total factor productivity (TFP) growth rates higher than those for manufacturing comes from a recent panel study on sectoral productivity growth in OECD and developing countries.[77] In this study, depending on the estimation method, the average growth rate for agricultural TFP in middle-income developing countries ranges from 1.78 to 2.91 (in % per year).

Other elements of simple dynamics include exogenous growth of labor supply, with skilled labor growing faster than unskilled labor, and investment driven capital accumulation.[78]

Equation (17) determines labor supply growth for the skilled workers (unskilled labor supplies are determined in equations (6) and (7)). It simply applies an exogenous assumption about the growth of labor supply, g^{ls}, to the labor supply shift parameter. Equation (18) updates population. Equations (19) and (20) are similar growth equations for land and the sector-specific resource, respectively.

$$\alpha_l^{ls} = (1 + g_l^{ls})\alpha_{l,-1}^{ls} \tag{17}$$

$$Pop = (1 + g^{Pop}) Pop_{-1} \tag{18}$$

$$Land = (1 + g^t) Land_{-1} \tag{19}$$

$$\gamma_i^{nr} = (1 + g_i^{nr})\gamma_{i,-1}^{nr} \tag{20}$$

Capital accumulation is based on the level of investment of the previous period less depreciation. Equation (21) represents the motion equation for capital growth, where δ is the rate of depreciation and KAP is the capital stock.

---

77 See Martin and Mitra (1999).
78 Note that public investment, in this version of the model, has no impact on production technology.

$$KAP = (1 - \delta)KAP_{-1} + XF_{ZIp,-1} \tag{21}$$

Other exogenous variables may require updating for the baseline. One obvious one is government expenditure. This is typically assumed to grow at the same rate as GDP:

$$\overline{XF}_{Gov} = (1 + g^y)\overline{XF}_{Gov,-1} \tag{22}$$

Other variables that have been updated include the various transfer variables, foreign savings, exogenous world prices (i.e. the terms of trade), and fiscal policies.

4.3.2. The micro model

The micro model is linked to the macro model through changes in the following set of endogenous (in the CGE model) variables: (a) changes in agricultural and non-agricultural labor income of unskilled labor (2 variables); (b) changes in labor income of skilled labor (1 variable); (c) changes in the sectoral (agriculture vs. non-agriculture) composition of the unskilled workforce (1 variable). In addition, we take into account that unskilled and skilled labor supplies grow at different rates. In the microsimulation, we do not produce a series of cross-sections through time, but only simulate one cross-section that reflects the cumulative changes in the aforementioned exogenous and endogenous variables between 2001 and 2015.

In accordance with the structure of the CGE model, the micro model treats skilled and unskilled labor differently and, in particular, simulates the decision to move from agriculture into non-agricultural sectors only for unskilled workers.

In the following, we first illustrate the equations to be estimated to serve as a basis for the microsimulation and we report and comment on some estimation results.[79] Then, we outline the microsimulation module that combines (static) reweighting methods to reflect the changes in the composition of the labor force, i.e. the unskilled/skilled labor ratio, and (dynamic) behavioral elements to simulate the sectoral movements and wage changes given by the CGE. We conclude this section by pointing towards possible shortcomings of the data and the methods applied.

---

79 The estimations are based on the 2001 PNAD. The sample includes 378 701 individuals in 112 558 households. The number of employed individuals used for the estimation of the income generation model is 166 646. Due to a relatively large number of missing income observations, labor incomes are imputed using simple OLS income regressions for different groups of employed individuals (urban/rural, agriculture/non-agriculture, worker/self-employed/employee). See Ferreira et al. (2001) for details on the PNAD dataset and the problems of using the PNAD income measure for poverty and distributional analysis.

First, we estimate sectoral mover-stayer models for unskilled heads and non-heads separately. For both heads and non-heads, we observe whether an individual has moved from agriculture into a non-agricultural sector. Our sample hence consists of those individuals who are still in agriculture and those who have moved out of agriculture within the last year.

In contrast to many other household surveys, the PNAD provides information on employment histories, which allows us to identify the movers out of agriculture and, very important for our undertaking, the characteristics of the movers at the time of moving. For all the movers we thus know, for example, which type of land right they had if they were self-employed before they moved out of agriculture. To our knowledge, this information has not been explored to date. The estimated model hence combines the idea of the mover-stayer model from the migration literature[80] with the approach to modeling occupational dynamics typically applied in income generation microsimulations.[81] In the latter approach, bi- or multinomial choice models are estimated on the entire population. In our case, this would imply comparing the characteristics of those in agriculture with those in non-agricultural sectors. Instead, the mover-stayer model compares the characteristics of only the movers with those of the stayers. This appears to be more appropriate in the current setting, as our goal is to simulate the transition from agriculture to non-agriculture.

Let *move* be a dichotomous variable that assumes a value of 1 if the individual has moved out of agriculture in the last year, and 0 if the individual has stayed in agriculture. As indicated by equation (23), an individual will move (*move* = 1) if the utility (*U*) associated to this choice is higher than the utility of staying in agriculture.[82] Otherwise, the individual will stay in agriculture (24).

$$move = 1 \ if \ U \ (move=1) > 0 \tag{23}$$

$$move = 0 \ otherwise. \tag{24}$$

As indicated by equations (25) and (26), the utility of moving depends on a set of explanatory variables X and a random error term ε. We hence assume a linear relationship between utility and the explanatory variables. The subscripts *msh* and

---

80 See for example Nakosteen and Zimmer (1980).

81 See for example Robilliard, Bourguignon, and Robinson (2002) and Bussolo and Lay (2005). The combination of retrospective information and choice models has been applied in microsimulation models e.g. to model fertility or schooling decisions. See Grimm (2005) for an application on Côte d'Ivoire.

82 The utility of staying in agriculture is assumed to be 0. This is typical identifying assumption of the logit.

msnh refer to heads and non-heads, respectively. They also serve to remind us that the parameters and variable vectors are from the mover-stayer (*ms*) model.[83]

$$U(move = 1)_{msh} = \alpha_{msh} + X_{msh}\beta_{msh} + \varepsilon_{msh} \qquad (25)$$

$$U(move = 1)_{msnh} = \alpha_{msnh} + X_{msnh}\beta_{msnh} + \varepsilon_{msnh} \qquad (26)$$

where X_{msh} includes an educational dummy for more than 10 years of schooling, age, a dummy that refers to own-consumption worker, an employment category to our knowledge unique to the PNAD that describes workers who are not self-employed, do not receive any monetary income, and work "for their own consumption"[84], two dummies that refer to the type of land right held by the self-employed in agriculture, one referring to a situation, in which the landowner agrees with the self-employed occupying the land and another to the self-employed owning the land, and a regional dummy for the northern region. X_{msnh} for the non-heads is a vector of similar variables, but some notable differences that will be discussed later in the regression results section. It consists of three educational dummies, experience (age-schooling-6), experience squared, a female dummy, a dummy for blacks, and the same employment category and land right dummies as before plus a dummy for non-remunerated family members or workers. Note that the reference group for the employment-related dummies are the wage-employed. In addition, the explanatory variables for the non-heads include a dummy for the household head being employed in a non-agricultural sector and another dummy for the head being a mover out of agriculture.

As we cannot observe the latent utility U, the parameters of the mover-stayer model will be estimated by maximum likelihood logit techniques, i.e. we estimate the models described by equations (27) and (28), where F denotes the cumulative density function of the logistic distribution.

$$\Pr ob(move_{msh} = 1 \mid X_{msh})_{msh} = F(\alpha_{msh} + X_{msh}\beta_{msh} + \varepsilon_{msh}) \qquad (27)$$

$$\Pr ob(move_{msnh} = 1 \mid X_{msnh})_{msnh} = F(\alpha_{msnh} + X_{msnh}\beta_{msnh} + \varepsilon_{msnh}) \qquad (28)$$

In addition to the sectoral choice model, Mincer wage/profit equations for unskilled labor in agriculture (the subscript *uagr*) and non-agriculture (*unagr*), and for skilled labor (*s*) are estimated:

---

83 We do not use a subscript for indicating individual observations in the exposition of the micromodel for illustrative purposes.
84 See Notas Metodológicas PNAD 2001.

$$\ln w_{uagr} = \alpha_{uagr} + X_{uagr}\beta_{uagr} + uw_{uagr} \tag{29}$$

$$\ln w_{unagr} = \alpha_{unagr} + X_{unagr}\beta_{unagr} + uw_{unagr} \tag{30}$$

$$\ln w_s = \alpha_s + X_s\beta_s + uw_s \tag{31}$$

where the explanatory variables in all three equations include years of education, experience, the corresponding squared terms, a female dummy and racial dummies. In addition, we include regional dummies that in equations (30) and (31) also differentiate between rural and urban areas. In the equation for the unskilled in agriculture (29), we introduce a dummy for being self-employed and the number of non-remunerated family members in order to capture their labor input. The wage/profit equations (29) to (31) are estimated using Ordinary Least Squares (OLS).

Some words on the choice of this specification are in order, as estimating the two wage equations for unskilled labor using OLS may appear problematic to the reader who is familiar with the concept of selectivity bias and is aware of the available econometric methods to deal with it. The reason for estimating two wage equations is based on the assumption that the wage-setting process in agriculture is different from the one in non-agricultural sectors; and the results of our regressions confirm this assumption. When estimating two separate equations we therefore might have to account for selectivity bias. Selectivity bias refers to a bias in the coefficients of the wage equations which arises as the coefficients do not merely reflect the returns to education, seniority, or the influence of the included dummies, but also the returns of being employed in (or selected into) the respective sector. For example, having a high level of education affects the sectoral choice, i.e. the earnings indirectly, as well as the earnings directly. Applying OLS to the estimation of two separate (sectoral) wage equations would result in coefficients that reflect both the indirect (selection) and the direct effects. Selection can also be interpreted in terms of having a kind of "comparative advantage" in the chosen sector, which is not explicitly accounted for but represented by the biased OLS coefficients. Econometricians often describe the concept of selectivity by noting that the selection into the respective sectors is non-random. It has become very common to correct for selectivity bias using the so-called Heckman correction or one of its many variants.

Many authors have warned against the indiscriminate use of the selectivity correction methods.[85] In line with this general skepticism, for reasons that have to do with the purpose of estimating the above equation, and due to practical estimation problems, we believe that correcting for selectivity bias is not necessary or may even lead to wrong results in the present context. The purpose of

---

85 See Johnston, Di Nardo (1997, pp. 449-450) for a short overview of the major problems involved and the citations there.

estimating the wage equations is to impute earnings for those who move between sectors. If we estimate the wage equation using OLS we implicitly assume that the returns to education and other characteristics of the individual include the indirect returns due to selection. We believe that this can be reasonably assumed, as an individual, for whom a wage is to be imputed, is actually selected into the corresponding sector.[86] In addition, estimating a selection model rendered inconsistent results. The only feasible estimation strategy would then have been to reduce the number of explanatory variables in the wage equation to include only one educational dummy for tertiary education with the remaining educational dummies to be only included in the selection equation.[87] This of course would have been highly unsatisfactory in terms of explaining the variation in earnings. These results are mainly owed to a combination of the following two factors. First, lower levels of education are highly significant in selecting an individual into agriculture. Second, there is little variation in these variables for those in non-agricultural sectors. In light of these theoretical and practical arguments we used OLS rather than Heckman correction procedures.

With few exceptions the explanatory variables of the mover-stayer models as well as in the wage/profit equations are significant at the 5 percent level.[88] The detailed regression results are reported in the App. Table 4.1 and App. Table 4.3, but here we just want to comment on some results that we find remarkable and consider of particular importance with regard to the simulation exercise.

The mover-stayer models appear to have some predictive power for the decision to move out of agriculture, as indicated for example the Pseudo R^2 of 0.07 for the heads' and 0.15 for the non-heads' mover-stayer model. It should be noted that measures of fit for logit models can only provide a rough indication of whether a model is adequate (Long and Freese 2001).

In the mover-stayer model for heads, one educational dummy for 10 or more years of schooling, turned out to have a significant positive influence on moving out of agriculture. Yet, we find a number of factors that negatively affect the choice of moving, among which age is the most important one. As we would expect, older individuals are less likely to move out of agriculture. The effect of a discrete change in age of some years is particularly strong for younger individuals. Working only for own-consumption also has quite a strong negative effect on the propensity to move out of agriculture. Many of these own-consumption workers are employed in the livestock sector and possibly even own livestock. In addition, if household heads own land or if they have an agreement with the landowner to occupy the land, they are more likely to stay in agriculture. Owning land or other agricultural production factors, such as livestock, hence acts as important barrier to

---

86 This assumption implies that there are no differences between individuals in terms of sectoral comparative advantages. If we estimated the wage equation correcting for selectivity, these differences would be reflected in the individual inverse Mills ratios.

87 These or similar problems of applications of the Heckman procedure are often noted in applied work. A case in point is Spatz (2004b).

88 Standard errors are adjusted for clustering.

intersectoral movements. Finally, household heads from the north are more likely to move out of agriculture, an interesting finding one might not necessarily expect, as the north is a region with a low share in agricultural employment.

As described above, the list of explanatory variables for non-heads is longer. The strongest determinant of moving out of agriculture is the dummy indicating whether the household head is employed in a non-agricultural sector. We can think of either a self-employed head being able to offer employment to other household members in a non-agricultural household enterprise or networks of a wage-employed head that facilitate finding non-agricultural employment for relatives. In addition, the choice of the household head to leave agriculture strongly influences the choice of the non-heads. Educational dummies for having finished primary and secondary education have a significant positive effect on the probability of moving out of agriculture. This effect is strongest for having finished primary education and declines somewhat for higher educational levels. The effect of a change in experience is much stronger than the effect of the corresponding change in the squared term. As in the case of the heads, the overall marginal effect of experience (including the squared term) declines with increasing experience. The subset of coefficients for educational dummies, experience, and squared experience can be interpreted as reflecting the earnings opportunities of an individual in non-agricultural employment. In other words, these five explanatory variables can be thought of as a reduced form representation of the wage differential between agricultural and non-agricultural activities. Accordingly, the coefficients for education can be seen to reflect decreasing returns to education for the movers and the results for experience appear to catch both the effect of age being a barrier to move out of agriculture as well as the typical seniority effect in earnings, i.e. increasing but marginally decreasing returns to experience. In a similar way, the significant and negative coefficients for racial dummies can be interpreted either or both as a direct barrier to non-agricultural employment and/or an indirect effect that works through more racial discrimination in non-agricultural employment than in agriculture.

Non-remunerated workers are less likely to move out of agriculture. This finding point towards the importance of externalities associated to this type of employment, as estimation results indicate that the income gains due to an additional household member engaged in the household farm are rather moderate (see App. Table 4.3). The coefficients of being an own-consumption worker or owning land are of the same sign as in the case of the heads and the changes in predicted probabilities due to a change in the dummy of equal magnitude.

In sum, the results for the heads show the barriers to moving out of agriculture, whereas the results for non-heads also illustrate the possible gains of such a move. Household heads appear to respond to wage differentials between agricultural and non-agricultural sectors to a lesser degree. They hence tend to be "trapped" in agricultural activities, possibly due to factor market imperfections. Their decision to stay or move however is of great importance for the decision of other household members.

The microsimulation involves three steps. First, households are reweighted in order to reflect the change in the skilled/unskilled labor ratio that results from different growth rates of these two types of labor over time. In a second step, unskilled labor moves out of agriculture until the new share of unskilled labor in agriculture given by the CGE is reproduced. Third, wages/profits are adjusted according to the CGE results taking into account the changes in the skill composition of the workforce as well as the sectoral movements of unskilled labor from agriculture into non-agricultural sectors.

The reweighting procedure basically increases the weight of skilled individuals and decreases the weight of unskilled individuals to reach a new given ratio of unskilled to skilled workers following an efficient information processing rule.[89] Let *weight* denote the old weight (normalized to 1), and *nweight* the new weight of individual i. As Robilliard and Robinson (2003), we estimate the new weights by minimizing the Kullback-Leibler cross-entropy measure of the distance between the new and the old weights

$$\text{Min} \sum_i nweight_i \cdot \ln\left(\frac{nweight_i}{weight_i}\right) \tag{32}$$

subject to the following constraints

$$\frac{\sum_i nweight_i \cdot u_i}{\sum_i nweight_i \cdot s_i} = \frac{lu \cdot (1 + g_u)}{ls \cdot (1 + g_s)} = \frac{lu^*}{ls^*} \tag{33}$$

$$\sum_i nweight_i = 1 \tag{34}$$

with u (s), a dummy variable for unskilled (skilled) individuals i, lu (ls), the initial unskilled (skilled) labor force, and g_u (g_s), the cumulative growth rate (between 2001 and 2015) of the unskilled (skilled) labor force. lu^* (ls^*) hence denotes the target value for the number of unskilled (skilled) labor. Equation (33) hence states that the new weights have to reflect the new skill composition (the ratio of unskilled to skilled workers) of the workforce. Equation (34) is the adding-up normalization constraint.

Note that this procedure gives new individual weights for just the employed population. Yet, for our purposes we need household weights for entire population.

---

89 For details on maximum entropy econometrics see Golan, Judge and Miller (1996). Robilliard and Robinson (2003) apply these methods to reweight household survey weights. They also provide a GAMS code for solving this type of problems.

To those households where one or more individuals are employed, we assign the mean of the new individual weights. Households without any employed members were given the old weight. Note that the resulting unskilled-skilled ratio under these "final" new weights is of course not exactly equal to the ratio imposed in the cross-entropy reweighting.[90] Since the workforce in agriculture is almost entirely unskilled (more than 95 percent), the share of the unskilled labor force in agriculture is only slightly lower under the new weights. We use these new weights throughout the following parts of the microsimulation.

The estimation of the sectoral choice logit model and the two wage equations provide the basis for the following steps in the simulation. In the second step, we apply the changes in the sectoral composition of the workforce from the CGE (from agricultural into non-agricultural sectors) to the microlevel. In the simulation, those individuals from agriculture with the highest propensity to move to non-agricultural sectors are chosen to leave agriculture. This propensity is simulated by calculating the linear prediction of the logit model and adding a simulated residual.

Equations (35) to (39) indicate how we move unskilled individuals out of agriculture. Let the index j refer to all unskilled individuals employed in the agricultural sector and i to all employed individuals. Note that the share of unskilled agricultural employment may change (and actually does, but only slightly) because of the introduction of the new weights at this stage and that move (not move*) is 0 for all j, as their observed choice is to stay in agriculture. Individuals move to non-agricultural sectors, i.e. move* equals 1, if the utility associated to the choice to move increases. Equations (38) and (39) illustrate that we increase the utility of moving by augmenting the constants $\hat{\alpha}_{msh}$ and $\hat{\alpha}_{msnh}$ by $\Delta\alpha_{msh}$ and $\Delta\alpha_{msnh}$, respectively, in order to make individuals move. Changes in the choices of the heads have an impact on the choices of the non-heads, as the head's choice enters the utility of the non-heads, indicated by X^*_{msnh}. The residuals $\hat{\varepsilon}^1_{msh}$ and $\hat{\varepsilon}^1_{msnh}$ are simulated such that the resulting utility is consistent with the observed outcome in the initial situation.[91] Using a Newton-Raphson algorithm, we augment the constants until equation (35) holds.

$$agrshare = \frac{\sum_j nweight_j - \sum_j move^*_j \cdot nweight_j}{\sum_i nweight_i} \tag{35}$$

90   We acknowledge that this is an ad-hoc procedure. In principle, it is possible to reweight all individuals respecting all necessary constraints. Yet, we consider the value added of this computationally quite expensive exercise too low.

91   There are also residuals associated to *move* = 0, which is why the residuals of *move* =1 have the superscript 1. The residuals are drawn from a Gumbel distribution (type I extreme value) conditional on the observed choice, as suggested by Bourguignon, Fournier, and Gurgand (1998).

with

$$move^* = 1 \text{ if } U^* (move^* = 1) > U^* (move^* = 0) \qquad (36)$$

$$move^* = 0 \text{ otherwise} \qquad (37)$$

and

$$U^*(move^* = 1)_{msh} = \left(\hat{\alpha}_{msh} + \Delta\alpha_{msh}\right) + X_{msh}\hat{\beta}_{msh} + \hat{\varepsilon}^1_{msh} \qquad (38)$$

$$U^*(move^* = 1)_{msnh} = \left(\hat{\alpha}_{msnh} + \Delta\alpha_{msnh}\right) + X^*_{msnh}\hat{\beta}_{msnh} + \hat{\varepsilon}^1_{msnh} \qquad (39)$$

In order to determine both $\Delta\alpha_{msh}$ and $\Delta\alpha_{msnh}$ we need another equation. We decided to fix the share of heads and non-heads movers so that equation (40) holds.

$$\frac{\sum_j move_j^{msh} \cdot weight_j}{\sum_j move_j^{msnh} \cdot weight_j} = \frac{\sum_j move^{*\,msh}_j \cdot nweight_j}{\sum_j move^{*\,msnh}_j \cdot nweight_j} \qquad (40)$$

After the assigning new weights and moving individuals out of agriculture, wages/profits need to be adjusted according to the CGE results in the third step of the simulation. We illustrate the procedure of adjusting the constants of the wage/profit equations for unskilled labor only.[92] Let $k=1,...,K$ be an index for unskilled individuals still employed in agriculture (excluding non-remunerated household members), $k=K+1,...,M$ for the movers, and, finally, $k=M+1,...,L$ for those unskilled in non-agricultural sectors who have been employed there before (again excluding non-remunerated household members). We assume that non-remunerated household members earn an own labor income once they move out of agriculture. In equations (42) and (44) we calculate the target values for average labor income in agricultural and non-agricultural sectors, $\tilde{w}_{uagr}$ and $\tilde{w}_{unagr}$, respectively, simply by multiplying initial average labor income by the growth rates g_{uagr} and g_{unagr} given by the CGE. These target values for the new distribution are reached by adjusting the constants in the wage/profit equations, as indicated by equations (43) and (45), taking into account the new weights that reflect the changed skill composition of the labor force. Note that for agriculture the procedure is slightly more complicated, as we also have to take into account that the dummy for agricultural self-employment as well as the number of non-remunerated family members might change, indicated by X^*_{uagr} in equation (43).

---

92 For skilled labor, the adjustment in the constant only needs to account for the changes in weights.

$$\tilde{w}_{uagr} = \frac{\sum_{k=1}^{M} w_{uagr_k} \cdot weight_k}{\sum_{k=1}^{M} weight_k} \cdot \left(1 + g_{uagr}\right) \tag{42}$$

$$\tilde{w}_{uagr} = \frac{\sum_{k=1}^{K} w_{uagr_k}^{*} \cdot nweight_k}{\sum_{k=1}^{K} nweight_k}$$

$$= \frac{\sum_{k=1}^{K} \exp\left((\alpha_{uagr} + \Delta\alpha_{uagr}) + X_{uagr}^{*} \hat{\beta}_{uagr} + \hat{uw}_{uagr} \right)_k \cdot nweight_k}{\sum_{k=1}^{K} nweight_k} \tag{43}$$

$$\tilde{w}_{unagr} = \frac{\sum_{l=M+1}^{L} w_{unagr_l} \cdot weight_l}{\sum_{l=M+1}^{L} weight_l} \cdot \left(1 + g_{unagr}\right) \tag{44}$$

$$\tilde{w}_{unagr} = \frac{\sum_{l=K+1}^{L} w_{uagr_l}^{*} \cdot nweight_l}{\sum_{l=K+1}^{L} nweight_l}$$

$$= \frac{\sum_{l=K+1}^{L} \exp\left((\alpha_{uagr} + \Delta\alpha_{uagr}) + X_{unagr} \hat{\beta}_{unagr} + \hat{uw}_{unagr} \right)_l \cdot nweight_l}{\sum_{l=K+1}^{L} nweight_l} \tag{45}$$

The unexplained wage $\hat{uw}_{unagr}$ for those who enter non-agriculture is calculated by taking the unexplained wage from agriculture and multiplying it by the ratio of the standard deviations of the residuals in the non-agricultural and agricultural sectors, respectively. For non-remunerated household members moving into non-agricultural sectors we simulate a residual.

In addition to labor income, we consider transfer and capital income as reported in the PNAD. Transfer income is scaled up or down with the GDP per capita growth rate and capital income with the change in the rental rate from the CGE model. The sum of all household members' individual incomes is divided by the number of household members to give the income per capita. We use regional poverty lines taking a R$ 80 per capita poverty line (in current 2001 prices) for urban Rio de Janeiro as a basis and adjusting for regional price differences following Paes de Barros (2004). The poverty lines are reported in App. Table 4.5.

Before we proceed to the results of our analysis, some shortcomings of the present approach have to be noted that will be addressed in future work. First, the household income generation process is of course much more complex than the proposed microsimulation model suggests. Many structural features of the Brazilian labor market, such as a high degree of informality in wage-employment and the important role of self-employment, are only accounted for rudimentarily. The major reason is that there is no point in modeling these labor market features on the micro level if they are not reflected in the CGE. Second, the data that we use to estimate the mover-stayer model may not only capture long-term transitions from agricultural into non-agricultural employment. Some of the movers may actually move into a non-agricultural job only temporarily, for example due to seasonal reasons. Third, doubts have emerged regarding the reliability of the information drawn from the PNAD, in particular on rural, informal sector, and capital income (World Bank 2003).

Finally, it may seem natural to assume that the sectoral movements are somehow related to physical migration from rural to urban areas either within or even between the Brazilian regions.[93] Traditionally, migration has acted as an important adjustment mechanism in Brazil. Nearly 40 percent of all Brazilians have migrated at one point in their lives (Fiess and Verner 2003). However, the data does not allow to link intersectoral movements to geographical migration. First, the migration-related questions of the PNAD unfortunately do not cover rural-urban migration. The available information is on whether an individual has moved between municipalities and/or between federal states. Second, using the information on migration in combination with the employment history from the PNAD 2001 suggests that only a minor share of about 12 percent of those leaving the agriculture actually migrates to another municipality. Approximately half of these migrants move to another federal state. In light of the importance of migration as an adjustment mechanism and the fact that the decline in agricultural employment is accompanied by a reduction in the rural population of equal magnitude, we think that these figures reflect data deficiencies rather than the Brazilian reality. It is quite likely that migrants are underrepresented in the PNAD. Therefore, we had to ignore the issue of geographical migration here due to the low share of migrants among the sectoral movers. Exploring these issues further and extending the model by linking structural change to geographical migration could prove a fruitful exercise, particularly in the Brazilian context.

---

93 This would of course add to the list of arguments why the labor market for the unskilled should be considered segmented.

4.4. Brazil in the next decade: How trade policy affects a Business as Usual scenario?

A central question of this chapter is assessing the poverty effects of trade policy reforms in the long run, when many structural adjustment forces shape the income generation process. Our starting point consists of using our CGE model to build a business as usual scenario depicting the evolution of the Brazilian economy in the next decade. This evolution should not be considered as a statistical forecast, but rather as a consistent "projection" of the economy in a future where inter-sectoral productivity growth differentials, skill upgrading, and migration of labor out of farming activities play major roles. This Business as Usual (BaU) projection is then contrasted with alternative scenarios where trade policy reforms are added. The following subsections, describe in details the macro and micro results for the BaU and trade scenarios.

4.4.1. The Business as Usual macro results

In the BaU scenario, real GDP for Brazil is projected to grow (from 2005 onwards) at the fairly sustained yearly rate of 3.3%; this is somewhat optimistic when compared with the recent two decades' (1980-2000) rate of 2%. This GDP growth performance is backed up by strong factor productivity growth rates. As explained above, productivity in the agriculture sector is factor neutral and its growth rate is exogenously set at 2.9% per year; in the non-farm sectors, growth of labor productivity is calibrated at 1.02% per year and growth of capital productivity at 0.82% per year.

These differences in productivity growth rates across sectors, combined with faster growth of the supply of skilled versus unskilled labor generate significant structural adjustments, in line with those observed for the last decade. The changes in the structure of labor markets, shown in table 4.2, are of particular relevance for poverty and income distribution trends. On the supply side, education increases the supply of skilled workers which is growing at a 2.0% annual rate versus a yearly 1.6% growth rate for the unskilled labor supply. Additionally, through out-migration, the supply of unskilled workers in agriculture is shrinking. Labor demand is affected by the following three factors: labor productivity in agriculture is exogenous and slightly higher than in the rest of the economy; income elasticity of private consumption is below one for agricultural commodities and above one for other commodities; and, finally, international prices for traded agricultural products are decreasing through time. These three factors concur in reducing demand for labor in agricultural sectors and are the key drivers for the migration towards the non-agricultural segment.

The described supply and demand trends are equilibrated by movements in the wages. In the time horizon considered here, the education premium is declining: real wages of the skilled increase at 1.3% annually. In non-agricultural sectors, wages for unskilled workers increase by the yearly rate of 0.9%, however this upward trend is dumped by migration. The reverse happens to agricultural wages which are boosted by the implied reduction of supply due to out-migration.

Table 4.2: Medium term labor market structural adjustments, 2001-2015

	Productivity of labor	Income elast. of demand	Employment Skilled	Unsk	Wages Skilled	Unsk	Unskilled Lab migration as % of: Sending Pop	Receiving Pop	Cumulative migratio 2001-2015
	Yearly gr	constant	Yearly growth rates				Yearly %		Millions
Agri	2.9	0.54			0.0	1.7	1.7		-4.0
Non-Agri	1.0	1.05			2.2	0.9		0.5	4.0
Economywide			2.0	1.7	1.3				

Source: Authors' calculations

As shown in Table 4.3 these structural trends result in a significant 5 percent points shrinking in the agricultural employment for unskilled combined with a reduction of the unskilled wage gap between agriculture and non-agriculture. Notice that the employment percent structure of this table is one of the key variables linking the macro and micro models.

Table 4.3: Employment shares and wage ratios in 2001 and 2015

	Employment % Skilled 2001	2015	Unskilled 2001	2015	Unskilled wages 2001	2015
Agri	4	3	27	22		
Non-Agri	96	97	73	78		
Ratio N-Agri/Agri					1.8	1.6

Source: Authors' calculations

The BaU's GDP and labor markets macro trends are linked to developments at the sectoral level (shown in Table 4.4). Output growth rates are slightly lower for the agricultural sectors than for the non-agricultural ones. Agriculture exports, due to falling primary commodity international prices, grow at a slightly lower pace than non-agriculture exports. Additionally, in agricultural sectors, employment of unskilled workers is stalled or reduced, whereas demand for skilled workers, whose wages are increasing at a contained pace, is increasing. Productivity gains dictate that less workers are needed to achieve the same output, and rising wages, in particular for unskilled workers, induce producers to substitute (although with a low level of substitution) skilled workers for unskilled ones. The rightmost panel of the table shows the relative sizes of sectors in terms of employment and the skill intensities of each sector. Services are the largest employers of both skilled and unskilled workers but, on average, they use skilled labor more intensively. Agriculture employs almost a third of unskilled workers and uses this factor quite intensively, whereas manufacturing labor intensities are in-between agriculture and services.

Table 4.4: BaU's output and trade sectoral growth rates, and employment intensities

	Annual average growth rates			Labor demand		Employment percentages			
				Labor demand		by sector		by skill	
	Output	Imports	Exports	Skilled	Unsk	Skilled	Unsk.	Skilled	Unsk
CerealGrains	3.2	2.5	2.3	0.3	0.1	0	5	2	98
OilSeeds	3.1	2.2	2.4	0.1	-0.1	0	1	6	94
RawSugar	3.2			0.2	0.1	0	1	4	96
OtherCrops	2.9	1.3	2.5	0.0	-0.1	1	12	3	97
Livestock	3.2	1.5		0.3	0.1	2	4	10	90
RawAnimalProducts	3.3	2.5	1.6	0.4	0.3	0	3	1	99
OilMinerals	3.3	3.0	2.9	1.5	1.7	0	0	15	85
LightManufacturing	3.3	0.8	3.7	1.0	1.2	1	2	16	84
AgriIndustriesExp	3.2	0.5	3.4	1.0	1.2	2	3	16	84
WoodProductsPaper	3.3	0.9	3.5	1.0	1.2	2	2	15	85
ChemicalsOilPr	3.3	1.8	2.9	1.1	1.3	2	1	30	70
MetalMineralProducts	3.5	1.8	3.3	1.2	1.4	2	2	17	83
MachineryEquipment	3.6	1.9	3.5	1.4	1.6	3	2	28	72
OtherServices	3.0	2.6	1.7	2.1	2.3	58	30	33	67
Construction	3.2			2.3	2.5	2	8	6	94
TradeCommunication	3.1	2.4	1.8	2.2	2.4	15	18	17	83
PublicServices	3.1	2.7	1.7	2.2	2.4	9	4	41	59
Agri	3.0	1.9	2.4		0.0	4	27	6	94
Non-Agri	3.2	2.0	3.1		2.2	96	73	26	74
Economywide	3.2	2.0	3.1	2.0		100	100	24	76

Source: Authors' calculations.

Note: The mapping of this table sectors and GTAP sectors is shown in App. Table 4.6 and App. Table 4.7.

4.4.2. Distributional and poverty results for the BaU

A moderate decrease in poverty between 2001 and 2015 results from micro-simulating the identified key structural trends on the Brazilian household data. Considering the full sample of all households, the headcount poverty ratio (P0) declines by about 6 percentage points (see Table 4.5). The reduction of the average normalized poverty gap (P1) and the poverty severity index (P2) indicates that those who remain poor move closer to the poverty line.[94] Inequality changes very

---

94 A short note on the interpretation of the reported poverty measures: The income-gap ratio, i.e. average income shortfall (of the poor) divided by the poverty line, can be calculated as P1/P0. This ratio is 0.4 for all households in our case, i.e. the perfectly targeted cash transfer needed to lift every poor person out of poverty is 40 percent of

little, as indicated by the 0.1 decrease in Gini coefficient (or as in the Theil or other inequality indices, not reported).

These average indices indicate that some progress in reducing aggregate poverty and inequality is achieved in a Business as Usual scenario, but these aggregate measures may conceal relevant distributional changes at a more disaggregated level. In fact, reaching stronger poverty reduction may require specific pro-poor policies which often rely, for their successful implementation, on more detailed information about disaggregated distributional effects.

A first obvious way to gather more detailed information is to analyze the poverty and inequality impacts separately for the agricultural and non-agricultural households.

Table 4.5: Poverty and inequality in the BaU scenario, by sectors

	All households		Non-agricultural		Agricultural households	
	2001 level	*2001-15 change*	*2001 level*	*2001-15 change*	*2001 level*	*2001-15 change*
PC income	314.9	1.5	351.9	1.2	148.3	2.3
Gini	58.6	-0.1	57.1	0.6	56.6	-0.7
P0	23.6	-5.6	18.6	-3.1	46.2	-13.8
P1	9.6	-3.0	7.1	-1.6	21.0	-8.0
P2	5.3	-1.8	3.7	-0.9	12.3	-5.2
Population %	100		81.8	3.3	18.2	-3.3
Contr. to P0			64.4	8.8	35.6	-8.8

Source: Authors' calculations.

Note: PC income is per capita income in 2001 R$ and the change is given as annual growth rate. All levels are in percent and changes in percentage points.

A household is classified as "agricultural" when its head and/or at least two of its members are employed in agriculture. In 2001, according to this classification, agricultural households accounted for 18.2 percent of the Brazilian population, poverty incidence among them almost reached 50 percent, and their contribution to total poverty was about 36 percent (see Table 4.5). Between 2001 and 2015, the share of agricultural households in the population shrinks by 3.3 percentage points following the decline in agricultural employment of more than 5 percentage points. Poverty among agricultural households falls by more than 13 percentage points, whereas poverty among non-agricultural households decreases by only 3.1 percent. Accordingly, the contribution of agricultural households to the headcount falls by almost 9 percentage points.

---

the poverty line times the number of the poor. Thus, 0.4 times the percentage point change in P0 (here 2.4) provides a percentage point change benchmark for evaluating the change in P1, as this would be the change in P1 that we would observe had the average income of the poor stayed constant while the headcount declined.

A more detailed analysis also shows that the lack of progress in aggregate inequality is due to the agricultural and non-agricultural groups' individual inequality indicators moving in opposite directions. Among non-agricultural households, inequality rises because skilled labor income, a major source of income for these households, grows faster than that of unskilled labor. Conversely, inequality among agricultural households falls, mainly because richer agricultural households earn a higher share of their income from non-agricultural unskilled labor and, in some cases, from skilled labor.

Figure 4.1: Growth incidence curves, BaU, all, agricultural, and non-agricultural households

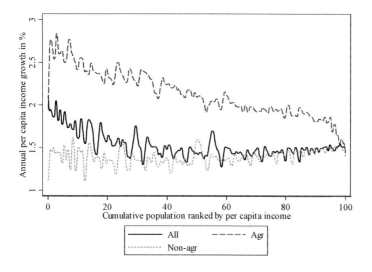

Source: Authors' calculations.

Another way of analyzing detailed distributional effects is to consider growth incidence curves. These curves plot per capita income growth at income percentiles (Ravallion and Chen 2003) and are shown in Figure 4.1 for all households as well as for the agricultural and non-agricultural groups.[95] Reflecting the increase in unskilled agricultural wages from the CGE model's results, per capita income growth is much higher for agricultural households. In addition, the agricultural growth incidence curve illustrates a strong pro-poor distributional shift, which reflects both the increase in agricultural labor incomes and the gains resulting from moving out of agriculture. These agricultural households specific distribution shifts also explain the pro-poor changes in the national distribution,

---

95 The household category, i.e. agricultural or non-agricultural household, is the category the household belonged to in the base year 2001.

since only minor distributional changes are registered in the non-agricultural distribution. However, richer non-agricultural households experience somewhat higher gains than poorer households. Non-agricultural poor household incomes increase by a meager 1 to 1.5 percent annually.

These more detailed analyses of the long term evolution of the Brazilian income distribution highlight the different roles played by changes in inequality and shifts in the growth rates of the average incomes. The following two relevant questions then arise: if the current (2001) distribution of income were to remain unchanged, how would additional growth help in reducing poverty? And, what is the role of the differential in the sectoral growth rates for agriculture and non-agriculture in reducing poverty?

Answering these questions requires performing two additional micro-simulations as follows. The first simulation generates a counterfactual distribution under the assumption that all incomes out of all sources grow by 1.5 percent annually. This implies shifting the entire income distribution "to the right" leaving its shape unchanged. Individuals do not change employment sectors and hence households retain their initial non-agricultural or agricultural classification. Results are presented in Table 4.6 and changes are given as percentage share of the BaU change (column I). In addition, we simulated a second counterfactual distribution for agricultural and non-agricultural households separately with per capita incomes of the respective household types growing with the BaU rates, i.e. by 1.3 percent annually for non-agricultural and 2.4 percent annually for the agricultural households (column II).

Table 4.6: Poverty and inequality in a distributionally neutral scenario

	All households			Non-agricultural households			Agricultural households		
	2001 level	% of BaU change I	% of BaU change II	2001 level	% of BaU change I	% of BaU change II	2001 level	% of BaU change I	% of BaU change II
PC income	314.9	100.0	100.0	351.9	117.7	100.0	148.3	65.7	100.0
P0	23.6	91.7	102.4	18.6	139.8	133.3	45.9	56.5	90.5
P1	9.6	90.9	97.7	7.1	132.5	119.7	20.8	61.9	93.2
P2	5.3	86.8	97.9	3.7	125.6	114.3	12.1	62.6	93.4

Source: Authors' calculations.

The comparison of the counterfactual simulations of the "completely" distributionally neutral (column I) and the "separately" neutral (column II) scenarios shows that the growth bias in favor of agricultural households is poverty reducing. Yet, the difference between the BaU and the completely neutral scenario does not seem too pronounced. This is due to the fact that poverty among non-agricultural households is reduced much more than in the BaU, where the income distribution among these households worsens. This "slight" worsening of the income distribution hence hampers quite strongly the potential of growth to reduce poverty among non-agricultural households. In addition, the differences between the two neutral scenarios for non-agricultural households illustrate that a 0.2 percentage point difference in annual growth rates for 14 years can make a difference in terms of poverty reduction. The last two columns of Table 4.6 show the importance of growth for reducing poverty among agricultural households as well. A 0.9 point percentage point difference in annual income growth rates for 14 years implies a reduction of about 5 percentage points less in the headcount over this time period. In contrast to what we see for non-agricultural households, the impact of the pro-poor distributional shift for agricultural households observed in the BaU is relatively small. In other words, had the income distribution among agricultural households not improved, growth would have reduced poverty by only little less.

The poverty reductions recorded in the BaU scenario are due the change in skill endowments, the increase in real factor prices, and inter-sectoral movements. A main advantage of micro-simulation techniques is their ability to decompose the total effect in different partial effects that can be attributed to single causes. A slight complication arises because different causes interact. The interaction arises because factor incomes increase at different rates in agricultural and non-agricultural sectors. By simulating counterfactual distributions, where only one cause at the time, or a combination of two of them, are included, it is possible to decompose the total effect into individual or joint (interactive) contributions.

Figure 4.2: Decomposition of poverty changes, BaU, all households

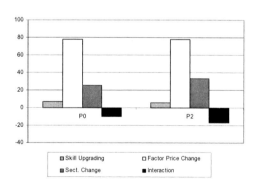

Source: Authors' calculations.

Note: The figure displays the contribution of the respective component to the total change in P0 and P2, respectively, in percent. The contributions add to 100. Contributions refer to reductions in the respective poverty indices.

Figure 4.2 displays the results of this decomposition. Factor price changes account for the largest share of total poverty reduction. The change in the skill composition of the workforce does not contribute much to poverty reduction, whereas the sectoral shifts are quite important, in particular for the poorer among the poor, as the higher contribution of the sectoral change component with regard to P2 indicates. This implies that households with members moving out of the agricultural sector escape poverty. We consider this issue in more detail later. The interaction component, which actually is a sum of distinct interaction components, hampers poverty reduction. Counterfactual simulations show that the interaction between sectoral movements and income changes is the most important one. It is negative since people move out of agriculture where their incomes would have increased much more than in non-agricultural sectors.

In sum, the distributional and poverty analysis suggests that the BaU scenario leads to relatively little poverty reduction. Agricultural households fare quite well and the poverty incidence and intensity among them is reduced quite substantially. Decomposition analyses show that sectoral change contributes quite significantly to poverty reduction, although income growth is the most important source of poverty reduction. Micro-accounting exercises underline the importance of growth for poverty reduction, but we also illustrate that slight increases in inequality can considerably reduce the poverty reduction potential of growth in the context of a high-inequality country, such as Brazil.

4.4.3. Macro results for the full liberalization and the Doha trade policy shocks

The trade shocks simulated in the dynamic CGE model consist of changes in Brazilian tariff protection against imports from the rest of the world and of exogenous changes of international prices of traded goods and export quantities demanded by foreigners.[96] The shocks are assumed to take place progressively through a gradual phasing-in starting in 2005 and lasting 6 years. Table 4.7 displays these shocks as percentage changes of the final year (2015) between the BaU and the trade reform scenarios. As part of the shock and to leave the government fiscal balance unchanged, tariff revenue losses are compensated by a lump sum transfer implemented as an increase in the direct taxes paid by households. This lump sum additional tax is the least distortionary instrument that can be readily used in our model, however, in practice, the Brazilian government may chose other forms of compensatory taxes which may alter relative prices and have significant income distribution effects.

---

96 It should be noted that to mimic the global model results for increased demand for Brazilian exports and changes in international prices, we introduce a downward sloping export demand function as shown in equation (1) above. During a shock, for obvious reasons, we cannot target both prices and quantities and the shock is implemented by modifying both the international price index *WPEindex* (the price shock) and the intercept α^{e}_{k} (the quantity shock). Our Brazil (single-country) model will then endogenously determine the quantity supplied.

Table 4.7: Trade shock – Tariff reductions and international prices changes

	Own tariff reductions			Change in import prices			Change in export prices		
	Full lib	Deep Doha	Weak Doha	Full lib	Deep Doha	Weak Doha	Full lib	Deep Doha	Weak Doha
CerealGrains	-100			8	2.0	2.1	16	5.9	6.0
OilSeeds	-100			6	2.5	2.5	14	4.8	4.9
RawSugar				2	0.9	1.0	14	5.3	5.4
OtherCrops	-100	0	0	2	0.9	0.9	13	4.7	4.8
Livestock	-100			2	1.0	1.1	25	9.7	9.8
RawAnimalProducts	-100			2	0.4	0.4	18	6.6	6.7
OilMinerals	-100	0		0	0.1	0.1	2	1.1	1.3
LightManufacturing	-100	-6	0	1	1.1	1.2	9	3.8	4.0
AgriIndustriesExp	-100	-4	-1	0	0.6	0.6	7	3.0	3.2
WoodProductsPaper	-100	-6	-2	0	0.0	0.0	4	1.8	2.0
ChemicalsOilPr	-100	-11	-3	-1	-0.1	0.0	3	1.4	1.7
MetalMineralProducts	-100	-6	-1	0	0.0	0.0	3	1.6	1.7
MachineryEquipment	-100	-7	-2	0	0.0	0.0	2	1.5	1.7
OtherServices				0	0.0	0.0	5	2.0	2.2
Construction				0	0.0	0.0	4	1.7	1.9
TradeCommunication				0	-0.1	-0.1	5	1.9	2.1
PublicServices				0	-0.1	-0.1	5	2.1	2.3
Agri	-100	0	0	5	1.5	1.5	14	4.8	4.9
Non-Agri	-100	-7	-2	0	0.0	0.1	4	1.9	2.1
Economywide	-100	-7	-2	0	0.1	0.1	5	2.2	2.4

Source: Authors' calculations.

The full liberalization scenario has the largest impacts: tariffs are completely eliminated and Brazil enjoys strong terms of trade gains; the other two shocks, representing two possible versions of the Doha negotiation outcomes, generate almost no own liberalization and fairly muted global prices effects. In order to fully appreciate their final effects, these shocks need to be mapped to the economic structure of Brazil. Table 4.8 presents this structure and helps in this regard. For instance, in the full liberalization scenario, export oriented sectors – those displaying high shares of export to domestic output – such as Oilseeds, Other Crops and the industrial sectors transforming agricultural products (*AgriIndustriesExp* which buys most of its inputs from agriculture) record considerable increases of their export prices. Conversely, import competing sectors, such as Chemicals and Oil derived products and capital goods, do not face high increases in their international prices. These combined export and import price movements result in fairly strong terms of trade gains, inducing significant reallocation of resources towards export oriented sectors. Additional push for this reallocation comes from Brazil's own liberalization which entails a reduction of the anti-export bias implicit in the higher protection rates for manufacturing of the initial tariff structure.

Table 4.8: Initial (year 2001) structure of the Brazilian economy

	Tariff rates	Sectoral imports	Imports / DomDem of comp	Sectoral output	Sectoral exports	Exports / Dom output
CerealGrains	7	1	15	1	0	1
OilSeeds	6	0	8	0	4	29
RawSugar	0	0	0	0	0	0
OtherCrops	9	2	3	4	8	7
Livestock	3	0	1	1	0	0
RawAnimalProducts	8	0	1	1	0	1
OilMinerals	4	7	33	1	7	25
LightManufacturing	17	4	5	5	3	2
AgriIndustriesExp	18	3	3	7	19	11
WoodProductsPaper	9	2	5	3	7	10
ChemicalsOilPr	9	15	10	9	8	3
MetalMineralProducts	12	5	6	5	13	11
MachineryEquipment	19	37	27	8	20	11
OtherServices	0	11	3	23	5	1
Construction	0	0	0	8	0	0
TradeCommunication	0	10	5	13	5	2
PublicServices	0	2	1	11	1	0
Agri	8	4	4	7	12	6
Non-Agri	11	96	6	93	88	4
Economywide	11	100	6	100	100	4

Source: Authors' calculations.

These effects are detailed in Table 4.9. The complete elimination of tariffs in the full liberalization case explains the large increase of imports (measured in volume) which, in the final year of this scenario, is 21% above the value in the same year of the BaU. Increases in imports of agricultural goods are much weaker: an aggregate 6% increase versus the 21% surge of the non-agriculture bundle. The combination of lower initial tariffs and stronger international price increases for agriculture, with respect to non-agriculture, explain the difference in import response of these two aggregate sectors. Given their very limited scope of tariff reduction, the Doha scenarios imply much more contained changes of imports.

With high elasticity of substitution in demand (currently set at 4), cheaper imports have the potential to displace domestic production, especially for those goods whose demand is fulfilled by a large share of foreign supply. For Brazil, this is the case for the Chemicals, and Capital goods sectors. In the full liberalization scenario, domestic production experiences significant market share losses in these sectors; however this is not happening in the Doha cases. The competition from cheaper imports is also reflected – again only for the full liberalization case – in the decline of prices of domestic output.

Table 4.9: *Brazil' structural adjustment, percent changes in the final year between BaU and trade shocks*

	Demand side								
	Import volumes			Domestic demand of dom products			Price of domestic output in dom mkts		
	Full lib	Deep Doha	Weak Doha	Full lib	Deep Doha	Weak Doha	Full lib	Deep Doha	Weak Doha
CerealGrains	-6	-3	-3	4	1	1	-2	1	1
OilSeeds	-18	-8	-7	5	1	1	-6	0	0
RawSugar				0	0	0	-2	1	1
OtherCrops	23	1	2	1	0	0	-1	1	1
Livestock	-4	1	1	3	1	1	-2	1	1
RawAnimalProducts	22	4	5	2	1	1	-2	1	1
OilMinerals	-6	0	1	1	-1	-1	-5	0	1
LightManufacturing	48	0	-3	0	1	1	-5	0	0
AgriIndustriesExp	59	2	1	0	0	0	-4	0	1
WoodProductsPaper	23	4	4	-1	0	0	-4	0	1
ChemicalsOilPr	18	5	3	-2	-1	0	-4	0	1
MetalMineralProducts	24	3	2	-4	-1	-1	-5	0	1
MachineryEquipment	42	5	3	-12	-2	-1	-6	0	1
OtherServices				1	0	0	-4	0	1
Construction	-14	2	3	0	0	0	-3	0	1
TradeCommunication	-12	2	3	0	0	0	-3	0	1
PublicServices	-13	2	3	0	0	0	-3	0	1
Agri	6	-2	-1	2	1	1	-2	1	1
Non-Agri	21	3	3	-1	0	0	-4	0	1
Economywide	21	3	3	-1	0	0	-4	0	1

Table 4.9 continued

| | Supply side | | | | | | | | |
| | Export volumes | | | Domestic output | | | Price of domestic | | |
	Full lib	Deep Doha	Weak Doha	Full lib	Deep Doha	Weak Doha	Full lib	Deep Doha	Weak Doha
CerealGrains	68	14	13	5	1	1	-2	1	1
OilSeeds	60	9	8	20	3	3	-3	1	1
RawSugar				0	0	0	-2	1	1
OtherCrops	6	-3	-3	1	0	0	-1	1	1
Livestock				3	1	1	-2	1	1
RawAnimalProducts	5	0	-1	2	1	1	-2	1	1
OilMinerals	26	2	1	7	0	0	-4	0	1
LightManufacturing	159	62	61	5	3	3	-4	0	1
AgriIndustriesExp	30	4	4	3	1	1	-4	1	1
WoodProductsPaper	11	-1	-1	0	0	0	-4	0	1
ChemicalsOilPr	9	-1	-1	-2	-1	0	-4	0	1
MetalMineralProducts	15	0	-1	-2	-1	-1	-4	0	1
MachineryEquipment	11	-1	-2	-10	-1	-1	-5	0	1
OtherServices				1	0	0	-4	0	1
Construction	8	-1	-1	0	0	0	-3	0	1
TradeCommunication	6	-1	-2	0	0	0	-3	0	1
PublicServices	7	-1	-2	0	0	0	-3	0	1
Agri	22	1	0	3	1	1	-2	1	1
Non-Agri	21	3	2	0	0	0	-4	0	1
Economywide	21	3	2	0	0	0	-4	0	1

Source: Authors' calculations.

These demand/imports side effects are linked to the supply response to which we now turn. For producers of exportable goods, the reduction of prices in local markets (ΔPd) combined with unchanged or rising export prices creates incentives to increase the share of sales destined to foreign markets. This export response (shown in the columns "Export Volumes") varies across sectors and it is linked to the pattern of Brazil's comparative advantage and to the increase in international prices. Brazil's comparative advantage can be ascertained by considering the export orientation (Exports / Dom Output) column in Table 4.8, which highlights three sectors in particular: Oilseeds, Other Crops, and the Agricultural transformation industry. These sectors – which also enjoy large jumps in their international price – experience export surges. Due to the generally positive export price shocks, other sectors join in an overall expansion of supply to foreign markets. Rising export sales more than offset, or at least compensate, reductions of domestic sales and lead to changes observed in the columns labeled "Domestic

Output". Finally output price changes (in the rightmost columns) are in between those of domestic prices and those of export prices for the simple reason that output prices are a combination (CET prices) of (generally) rising export prices and domestic prices.

As for the demand side, similar across-scenarios differences are observed for the supply side. In particular, given the closure rule for the foreign market, economy wide increases of import volumes are balanced by a comparable increase in exports.[97]

In summary, trade reforms promote a production structure specialized towards exportables, which in Brazil is translated in a specialization towards primary or agricultural transformation sectors. This agriculture export-led boom is fully achieved only in the full liberalization scenario, given its stronger price changes and the elimination of tariffs.[98]

The full liberalization and the two Doha scenarios entail trade policy reforms that combine, in different proportions, domestic tariff abatement with external price and quantity shocks. It has been shown that, in most situations, unilateral liberalization is beneficial; however it may be of interest, especially from a negotiation point of view, to decompose the total effect and ascertain the shares attributable to domestic liberalization and to external shocks. Given the interactions between Brazilian domestic policies and the Rest of the World (ROW) policies, a decomposition exercise is path dependent, therefore the shares attributed to one set of policy or the other will differ according to the choice in their sequencing.

For three key variables, Table 4.10 shows the effects of the total and partial shocks as indices calculated on the levels reached in the final year, with the final year for the BaU equal to 100. In the case of the full liberalization scenario and across all variables, own liberalization accounts for a large share of the total shock. Imports in agriculture actually increase more in the partial own liberalization shock than in the combined shock, given that the external shock drives international agricultural prices up. The reduction of the mentioned anti-(agriculture-)export bias implicit in the initial protection, is also explaining the large share of export and real GDP effects accounted by the own liberalization shock.

---

97 Due to the closure rule of the external account, namely the fixing of foreign savings, and the full employment assumption, the slightly lower expansion of the volumes of exports, with respect to import volumes is compensated with a real exchange rate appreciation which originates from rising domestic resource costs.

98 It should be stressed that in our model trade opening only produces allocative efficiency gains and not other, potentially much stronger, dynamic productivity gains.

Table 4.10: Effects on imports, exports and real GDP due to combined or partial
shock (Indices, BaU = 100 in 2015)

| | Demand side | | | Supply side | | | "Welfare" | | |
| | Import volumes | | | Export volumes | | | Real GDP | | |
	Full lib	Deep Doha	Weak Doha	Full lib	Deep Doha	Weak Doha	Full lib	Deep Doha	Weak Doha
Combined (Own + Rest of the world liberalization) shock --- BaU = 100									
Agri	105.7	98.3	99.1	122.4	100.7	100.2	102.9	100.0	99.9
Non-Agri	121.3	103.3	102.7	121.0	102.7	102.0	100.1	100.0	100.0
Economywide	120.8	103.1	102.5	121.2	102.5	101.8	100.2	100.0	100.0
Own shock --- BaU = 100									
Agri	107.3	98.9	99.8	114.5	100.8	100.2	102.0	100.2	100.0
Non-Agri	113.1	100.8	100.2	116.6	101.0	100.3	100.2	100.0	100.0
Economywide	112.9	100.8	100.2	116.4	101.0	100.3	100.3	100.0	100.0
Rest of the world shock --- BaU = 100									
Agri	96.8	99.4	99.4	107.1	99.9	99.9	101.0	99.8	99.8
Non-Agri	107.5	102.4	102.4	104.2	101.7	101.7	99.9	100.0	100.0
Economywide	107.1	102.3	102.3	104.4	101.5	101.6	100.0	100.0	100.0

Source: Authors' calculations.

Note: For each variable, these indices are calculated as the ratio of the level in the trade
scenarios to that of the BaU scenario for the last year (2015) and multiplied by 100.

Decomposition results for the Doha scenarios are less clear cut. The magnitudes
of the shocks are much smaller, however even the very low levels of domestic
tariff abatement seem to matter for the final result. A relevant policy lesson
emerges from the comparison of the two partial shocks panels of Table 4.10: a
passive non reciprocating attitude may bring some advantages; however these are
quite limited, even in the extreme case where every one in the world but Brazil
implements full liberalization. In fact, these externally-induced benefits may be
greatly enhanced by an active domestic liberalization reform.

For their poverty and income distribution implications, changes in factors'
markets are the most important aspect of the structural adjustment caused by trade
reform. Changes in wages and sectoral employment are linked to changes of goods
prices through the production technology and the functioning of the factor
markets. Different production technologies are approximated by different factor's
intensities across sectors, as shown in Table 4.4, and labor markets function so as
to mimic realistic adjustment possibilities: skilled workers can freely move across
all sectors, whereas unskilled ones face two segmented markets and can just
imperfectly migrate from the agricultural to the non agricultural segment.

Table 4.11: Factor markets effects

	Employment		Wages		Cumulative migration 2001-2015	Unskilled employment 2015
	Skilled	Unskilled	Skilled	Unskilled	Millions	%
	Yearly growth rates		Yearly growth rates			
Business as usual:						
Agri		0.02		1.68	-4.04	21.51
Non-Agri		2.20		0.91	4.04	78.49
Economywide	2.0	1.7	1.26			
Full liberalization:						
Agri		0.18		2.10	-3.71	21.99
Non-Agri		2.15		1.07	3.71	78.01
Economywide	2.0	1.7	1.32			
Doha:						
Agri		0.06		1.78	-3.96	21.64
Non-Agri		2.19		0.93	3.96	78.36
Economywide	2.0	1.7	1.27			

Source: Authors' calculations.

Table 4.11 highlights how trade shocks affect labor market structural adjustments. Due to its agriculture boom and its increased demand for "agricultural" factors of production, the full trade liberalization induces a significant increase in the wage rate for unskilled workers. When compared with the BaU, the yearly rate of growth of wage of unskilled workers in agriculture is 0.4 percentage points higher, and this higher rate accounts for a cumulative 14 year growth of 34% much higher than the cumulative growth of 26% in the BaU. Given this wage incentive, migration decreases and about 340 thousands workers who were moving out of agriculture in the BaU scenario do not switch activity in the full liberalization case. This has some effect on the aggregate distribution of unskilled workers between agriculture and non-agriculture, as shown in the last column of Table 4.11.

As far as the Doha scenarios are concerned, negligible effects are recorded for the employment structure and some weak wage increase is observed for unskilled in agriculture.

4.4.4. Trade scenarios' distributional and poverty results

Two fundamental results emerge from analyzing the micro impacts of the trade scenarios. Firstly, our initial hypothesis that trade liberalization, by working against the "natural" forces of structural change, might weaken long term trends of poverty reduction has been discarded. Although less people migrate towards higher paid non-agricultural jobs, mainly through increased agricultural incomes, poverty is further reduced in the trade liberalization scenarios. However, and this is the second fundamental result, trade reform as envisaged in the current Doha scenarios – but even in the hypothetical full liberalization one – is not of great help in the fight against poverty and its complete eradication needs additional more targeted and possibly more costly interventions.

These two sets of results are clearly illustrated by Table 4.12, which shows the poverty and distributional outcomes as percentage point differences between the trade scenarios and the BaU scenario for the final (2015) year: the full liberalization scenario leads to a further reduction in the headcount poverty index of 0.5 percentage points, whereas for deep Doha scenario the effects are almost negligible.[99] Similarly the Gini index is reduced by 0.2 and 0.1 percentage points in the full liberalization and deep Doha scenarios.

Table 4.12: Poverty and Distributional Impact of Trade, all households

	BaU 2015	% point diff. Doha	% point diff. Full
Gini	58.5	-0.1	-0.2
P0	18.0	-0.2	-0.5
P1	6.6	-0.1	-0.2
P2	3.5	0.0	-0.1

Source: Authors' calculations.

As for the BaU scenario, a thorough assessment of the trade scenarios needs to go beyond these aggregate indicators and should rely on more disaggregate poverty and distributional analyses. In search of trade-induced poverty effects, the remaining part of this section considers an array of indicators, from growth incidence curves to poverty statistics estimated on specific sub samples. In particular poverty and distributional impacts are separately measured for the agricultural and non-agricultural groups, the movers and stayers, the rural and urban populations, the regional samples, and the groupings obtained by educational attainment, by land ownership, and by occupational status.

Figure 4.3 shows the growth incidence curves for the poorest thirty percent of all households under the three scenarios. The curve for the deep Doha scenario lies slightly above the BaU curve. The full liberalization reform also shifts the whole curve upwards, however this shift is larger than that of the Doha case, and it seems to favor the poorest among the poor; in other words, full liberalization appears to induce an additional pro-poor distributional shift.

---

99 Given that the weak Doha scenario does not produce any visible results, in this section we just report results for the full liberalization and the deep Doha scenarios.

Figure 4.3: Growth incidence curves for the BaU and Trade scenarios, poorest 30 percent of all households

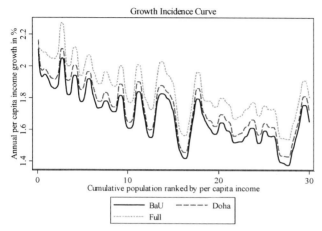

Source: Authors' calculations.

Table 4.13 shows the sectorally disaggregated results. Inequality for all households falls due to decreased inequality among agricultural households and lower inequality increase among non-agricultural households, although inequality between these two groups may have risen somewhat. Despite declining inequality and slightly higher per capita income growth, poverty reduction for agricultural households barely changes and this is due, as shown below, by the lower migration levels induced by the trade shocks. Indeed, in the deep Doha scenario the reduction in the population share of agricultural households is only very slightly below that achieved in the BaU. More remarkable is the additional poverty reduction for non-agricultural households that can largely be explained by the lower increase in inequality, as per capita income growth is only marginally higher.

Table 4.13: Poverty and inequality in the Doha scenario, by sector

	All households			Non-agricultural households			Agricultural households		
	2001 levels	*2001-15 changes*	*% of BaU change*	*2001 levels*	*2001-15 changes*	*% of BaU change*	*2001 levels*	*2001-15 changes*	*% of BaU change*
PC income	314.9	1.5	101.5	351.9	1.3	102.1	148.3	2.4	101.3
Gini	58.6	-0.2	194.4	57.1	0.5	81.8	56.6	-0.8	111.5
P0	23.6	-5.8	103.4	18.6	-3.3	106.5	46.2	-14.0	101.5
P1	9.6	-3.1	102.7	7.1	-1.6	104.6	21.0	-8.2	102.1
P2	5.3	-1.9	102.5	3.7	-0.9	104.3	12.3	-5.3	102.0
Population %	100.0			81.8	3.2	98.3	18.2	-3.2	98.3
Contr. to P0				64.4	8.6	96.0	35.6	-8.6	96.0

Source: Authors' calculations.

Given its larger price and quantities shocks, the full liberalization scenario yields more significant poverty changes, as shown in Table 4.14. In contrast to the Doha scenario, agricultural households gain considerably from full liberalization and their headcount index is reduced by almost 1.5 percentage points. This sector specific income gains more than compensate the further (albeit small) reduction of agricultural out-migration.

For non-agricultural households, the full liberalization scenario improves the income distribution, the Gini increases by only 72 percent of the increase recorded in the BaU. Growth is only slightly higher for this group of households but, as shown above, minor distributional shifts accompanied by slightly higher growth can result in significant poverty reduction.

Table 4.14: Poverty and inequality in the Full scenario, by sector

	All households			Non-agricultural			Agricultural households		
	2001 levels	*2001-15 changes*	*% of BaU change*	*2001 levels*	*2001-15 changes*	*% of BaU change*	*2001 levels*	*2001-15 changes*	*% of BaU change*
PC income	314.9	1.6	106.4	351.9	1.3	106.8	148.3	2.6	109.8
Gini	58.6	-0.3	312.2	57.1	0.5	72.0	56.6	-0.9	117.0
P0	23.6	-6.1	109.2	18.6	-3.6	116.3	46.2	-14.9	108.0
P1	9.6	-3.2	108.2	7.1	-1.8	113.7	21.0	-8.6	107.4
P2	5.3	-1.9	107.8	3.7	-1.0	113.0	12.3	-5.6	107.2
Population %	100.0			81.8	3.1	93.0	18.2	-3.1	93.0
Contr. to P0				64.4	8.4	96.0	35.6	-7.6	96.0

Source: Authors' calculations.

Trade shocks simultaneously increase agricultural incomes and reduce inter-sectoral migration and how these two contrasting forces affect poverty outcome depends on the income levels (and therefore on the socio-economic characteristics) of those who decide to stay instead of moving. The next set of tables sheds some light on this issue.

Table 4.15 shows the poverty levels and changes under the BaU and the trade scenarios for agricultural households who *remained* in agriculture. First consider the BaU case. Having identified those households that will not move, it is possible to calculate the headcount for this group in the initial year (2001): their headcount is equal to 44.1% more than 2 percentage points below the 46.2 level[100] calculated for all 2001 (stayer and potential mover) agricultural households. This lower *level* of poverty implies that moving households are on average poorer than those who remain in agriculture. Accordingly, the *changes* in P0 are 12.1 instead of 13.7 percentage points. In 2015, about 15 percent of the population still live in

---

100 Shown in Table 4.5.

agricultural households.[101] The agricultural expansion following trade liberalization has only a minor effect on agricultural employment, by far not enough to offset the reduction in agricultural employment from the BaU. Accordingly, the change of the share of agricultural households due to trade liberalization is only minor, in particular for the Doha scenario. Yet, when translated in actual migrating individuals, this small share change means that almost four hundred thousand individuals – who would have become members of non-agricultural households in the BaU – in the full liberalization scenario remain in agricultural households. Despite the fact that these "potential mover households" are on average poorer than the typical "stayer household", as we illustrate below, poverty among agricultural households decreases compared to the BaU. The poor stayers hence gain under both trade scenarios although this gain is almost negligible for the Doha scenario.

Table 4.15: Poverty impact of trade, agri stayers

| | | Households remaining in agri | | |
	2001 levels	BaU 2001-15 changes	Doha % of BaU change	Full % of BaU change
P0	44.1	-11.7	101.7	109.5
P1	20.0	-7.0	102.4	108.5
P2	11.7	-4.6	102.3	108.2
Population %		14.9	100.4	101.5

Source: Authors' calculations.

As could be indirectly inferred from the analysis of the stayers, the group of the movers should experience the largest welfare gains. Indeed as illustrated in Table 4.16, in the BaU agricultural households who become non-agricultural households record a 22.4 percentage points reduction in their headcount index, down from a considerably high, especially in comparison to the stayers group, initial level of 56.6 percent.

This outcome could not be derived straightforwardly from the estimation of the migration choice. In fact, the estimations showed that potential migrants were found to be poorer, in particular landless, heads, but also better educated, hence less poor, non-heads. The explicit quantitative measurements allowed by micro-simulation were needed to highlight the poverty reducing role of changes in the sectoral composition of employment.

---

101 The initial poverty levels among those who stay in agriculture under the trade scenarios are almost identical to the initial levels among the BaU stayers, so we decided not to report them. The same holds for the movers, for whom we report results later.

The observed poverty reduction under the trade scenarios is of a moderate additional increase. This is due to the income increases trade reforms induce in the non-agriculture sectors, but also because the fewer households that still move out of agriculture under the trade scenarios are actually poorer.

Table 4.16: Poverty impact of trade, sectoral movers

	Agri households who have become non-agri			
	2001 levels	BaU 2001-15 changes	Doha % of BaU change	Full % of BaU change
P0	56.6	-22.4	105.1	108.2
P1	26.0	-14.0	102.0	105.4
P2	15.2	-9.4	101.7	105.1
Population %		3.1	98.0	92.5

Source: Authors' calculations.

One final category needs to be examined: the non-agricultural stayers. Representing 80 percent of the population, this is a large group; however, given the negligible migration out of the non-agricultural sector observed in the data, this group is explicitly excluded from the migration choice. For these households, the full liberalization brings about an additional reduction in the headcount of 0.4 percentage points, and through its favorable impact on non-agricultural unskilled wages the Doha scenario, too, makes a small but noticeable difference.

Table 4.17: Poverty impact of trade, non-agri stayers

	Non-agri households before and after			
	2001 levels	BaU 2001-15 changes	Doha % of BaU change	Full % of BaU change
P0	18.6	-3.8	104.0	110.7
P1	7.1	-1.8	103.3	109.8
P2	3.7	-1.0	103.2	109.5
Population %	82.4			

Source: Authors' calculations.

Up to this point, the disaggregated analysis of the poverty impacts has been based on sectoral affiliation and thus it has been possible to link it directly to the sectoral results generated by the CGE model. However, additional policy relevant criteria can be used to identify other groups of households and to evaluate their specific trade induced poverty effects. In particular, we conduct impact analyses for rural and urban areas, by regions, by land ownership, by educational level and by occupation. Obviously, all these criteria are somehow correlated to basic categories (and variables) included in the CGE model, for example the educational level is linked to the skilled/unskilled factor types, or the region to the prevalence of agricultural employment. It should be noted that the criteria are not included in the CGE analysis. Yet, by using the full household survey information we can generate impact profiles where household are grouped according to poverty and distributionally relevant correlates.

Table 4.18: Poverty and inequality impact of trade, urban and rural

	Urban				Rural			
	2001 levels	*BaU 2001-15 changes*	*Doha % of BaU change*	*Full % of BaU change*	*2001 levels*	*BaU 2001-15 changes*	*Doha % of BaU change*	*Full % of BaU change*
P0	19.6	-4.0	103.8	112.2	44.4	-12.1	103.1	108.2
P1	7.6	-2.0	103.2	110.1	20.1	-7.1	102.5	108.2
P2	4.0	-1.2	103.0	109.5	11.7	-4.7	102.3	107.7
Population %	83.7	1.3	99.5	93.2	16.3	-1.3	99.5	93.2
Contr. to P0	69.4	3.9	96.6	35.5	30.6	-3.7	102.3	119.8

Source: Authors' calculations.

Table 4.18 shows the poverty impact of trade by urban or rural residence. Interestingly, the share of urban households in 2001 (83.7 percent) is even higher, although not much, than the share of non-agricultural households (81.8 percent). Quite some households live in urban areas, very likely in urban peripheries, and earn their living primarily from agricultural wage-employment. Actually, only 66 percent of the agricultural households live in rural areas, while 5 percent of the non-agricultural households live in rural areas. The micro-simulations that generate the results of Table 4.18 also take into account rural-urban migration by assuming that households migrate to urban areas if *all* employed household members leave agriculture. In the BaU, this causes the rural population to decline by 1.3 percentage points. The urban population accounts for almost 70 percent of the Brazilian poor in 2001 and this share rises in the BaU by 3.9 percentage points. Urban poverty declines under both trade scenarios with the decline being stronger under the full liberalization scenario. The Doha scenario hardly affects rural poverty, but full liberalization decreases the rural headcount by an additional percentage point. Some simple calculations can give some more meaning to these figures: The 0.5 percentage point difference in P0 in the full liberalization scenario means that approx. 135 000 people are lifted out of poverty.[102] The 1 percentage point difference implied by the full liberalization scenario reduces the number of poor people in rural areas by approx. 115 000. Considering the very small increase in non-agricultural unskilled wages this may be somewhat surprising, but it is the urban concentration that drives this result. Some more growth in urban areas lifts more people out of poverty than very high agricultural growth.

---

102 To put these absolute numbers into perspective it should be noted that the Brazilian population in 2001 was approximately 165 million, of which 39 million were poor (27 million in urban and 12 million in rural areas).

Table 4.19: Poverty impact of trade, by region

Region	2001 initial levels			2015		
	Population %	P0	% contr. to P0	BaU 2001-15 P0 change	Doha % of BaU P0 change	Full % of BaU P0 change
North	5.7	34.0	8.2	-7.9	101.0	107.7
Northeast	28.5	45.4	54.8	-9.3	102.6	109.5
Southeast	43.5	12.4	22.8	-3.7	101.9	107.9
South	15.2	14.7	9.5	-4.6	101.4	107.8
Center-West	7.1	16.0	4.8	-5.0	119.4	121.3

Source: Authors' calculations.

Due to the regional differences both in factor endowments and specialization patterns, we might expect poverty reduction patterns to differ substantially between the regions for the BaU as well as for the trade shocks. The reduction in the headcount for the BaU confirms this expectation, as poverty declines more strongly in the Northeast, South, and Center-West, the regions with the highest shares in agricultural employment. The Doha round has negligible effects across all regions although the figures in Table 4.19 suggest a different story for the Center-West. Yet, a look at the changes of P1 and P2 (not reported) demonstrates that this strong effect is due to many households being just below the poverty line in this region.[103] The Northeast, the region with the highest incidence of poverty where more than 50 percent of the Brazilian poor reside, benefits most from the Doha liberalization and about 50 000 individuals are lifted out of poverty in this region. In the same region, full liberalization helps about 175 000 individuals to escape poverty. The poor in the North, another region with worryingly high poverty rates, gain relatively little from trade liberalization, whereas poverty in the South as well as in the Center-West decreases quite substantially due to the importance of agricultural income for the poor in these regions.

Table 4.20 shows the poverty changes for landowners and agricultural households who do not own land separately. The landowning households account for approximately 40 percent of the population in agricultural households. The differences between the two groups of agricultural households are quite striking. The poverty incidence among landowning households is much lower; the difference is more than 10 percentage points. Poverty decreases quite substantially for both groups in the BaU. Note that we only consider households who stay in agriculture. Poor households who do not own land benefit little from the Doha round, but full liberalization brings about an additional decrease of more than 1 percentage point in the headcount (affecting almost 100 000 individuals). The

---

103 This is a case that illustrates why we usually report not only the headcount index, as this indicator can be quite misleading in some instances.

Table 4.20: Poverty impact of trade, agricultural stayers by owning land

	Landowner households				No land owning households			
	2001 levels	*BaU 2001-15 changes*	*Doha % of BaU change*	*Full % of BaU change*	*2001 levels*	*BaU 2001-15 changes*	*Doha % of BaU change*	*Full % of BaU change*
P0	37.1	-10.5	101.7	108.0	48.5	-12.5	101.9	110.6
P1	16.6	-6.2	102.7	109.1	22.2	-7.4	102.3	108.4
P2	9.5	-3.9	102.7	109.4	13.1	-5.0	102.2	107.8
Population %	38.4				61.6			

Source: Authors' calculations.

reason why they benefit more from both trade scenarios is that they are more specialized in agricultural income. This is not necessarily what one would expect, but it may well be that owning land provides the resources to set up a small non-agricultural business. Noteworthy is the finding that under both trade scenarios poverty gap as well as severity index decrease stronger than the headcount in terms of the BaU change. This again has to do with the specialization of households. The poorer landowning households derive a higher share of their income from agriculture whereas the richer households (at least among the poor) earn a higher share of income from non-agricultural activities.

Table 4.21: Poverty impact of trade, by educational levels

	2001 initial levels			2015			
Hh. average schooling	*Popula-tion %*	*P0*	*% contr. to P0*	*Popula-tion %*	*BaU 2001-15 P0 change*	*Doha % of BaU P0 change*	*Full % of BaU P0 change*
<= 3	16.2	52.3	35.9	16.0	-10.7	103.5	111.5
<=5	16.9	36.0	25.7	16.6	-9.1	102.9	109.9
<=8	20.9	21.1	18.7	20.7	-5.6	105.0	111.5
<=10	12.9	11.3	6.2	12.9	-2.9	104.6	111.3
>=11	33.1	9.6	13.5	33.7	-2.0	101.7	104.6

Source: Authors' calculations.

As Table 4.21 indicates, the educational level of the households is an important determinant of poverty. The headcount among households with 3 or less average years of schooling of the employed household members is well above 50 percent. This group accounts for 16.2 percent of the population but for more than a third of the poor. The poverty incidence among households with 4 or 5 years of schooling is 15 percentage points lower. For both groups with ten or more years of average schooling, the headcount is about 10 percent. The Doha round does not appear to be particularly helpful for those with little educational endowment. Yet, the full liberalization scenario again leads to a substantial additional reduction in poverty.

Finally, we analyze the poverty impact of trade reform by occupational groups. In Table 4.22, we differentiate between wage-employed, self-employed and households with members engaged in both types of employment in agricultural and non-agricultural activities, respectively.[104] In addition, there are households with no employed household member. One out of five poor people in Brazil comes from a self-employed agricultural household, and the agricultural wage-employed households are almost equally poor. In non-agricultural households, the difference between self-employed and wage-employed households in terms of poverty is not too pronounced. Due to their high share in the population, non-agricultural wage-employed households account for more than a third of the Brazilian poor. Poverty rates are significantly lower for households who derive their income from both wage-and self-employment. Under the Doha scenario, all non-agricultural household groups gain, whereas there are only minor gains for agricultural households. As noted above, full liberalization however helps both agricultural and non-agricultural households. Interestingly, poverty in non-agricultural activities declines more among the self-employed, whereas in agricultural activities the decline is stronger for the wage-employed. As in the case of households who do not own land, the agricultural wage-employed households derive more income from agricultural unskilled labor than agricultural self-employed households. For non-agricultural households, it is the greater importance of skilled income for the wage-employed that makes poverty decline less strongly for this group.

Table 4.22: Poverty impact of trade, by occupation

	2001 initial levels			BaU 2001-15		Doha 2001-15		Full 2001-15	
	Popula-tion %	*P0*	*% contr. to P0*	*Popula-tion % change*	*P0 change*	*Popula-tion % change*	*% of BaU P0 change*	*Popula-tion % change*	*% of BaU P0 change*
Agri wage-empl.	5.6	46.2	11.0	-1.5	-14.3	-1.5	101.5	-1.4	111.2
Agri self-empl.	10.2	48.0	20.7	-1.3	-13.7	-1.3	101.4	-1.2	106.7
Agri both	2.4	38.8	3.9	-0.5	-14.1	-0.5	101.3	-0.5	105.5
Not empl.	7.8	27.4	9.1	0.0	-4.3	0.0	100.0	0.0	100.0
Non-agri wage	48.5	17.2	35.3	1.6	-3.1	1.6	107.2	1.5	117.4
Non-agri self	15.9	22.7	15.3	1.1	-2.9	1.1	107.9	1.1	121.0
Non-agri both	9.6	11.5	4.7	0.6	-2.3	0.6	108.0	0.5	123.4

Source: Authors' calculations.

To sum up, the poverty changes under the deep Doha scenario are rather moderate and disappointing. With one exception, our analyses do not detect a particularly favorable effect on any of the poor and vulnerable groups that we have identified. This one exception is that the Doha scenario very slightly appears to favor the Northeast. Overall, income growth under the Doha scenario favors non-

---

104 If the number of self-employed household members is greater than the number of wage-employed members, the household is considered self-employed, and vice versa. Are the numbers equal, the households falls under the "both" category.

agricultural activities and, accordingly, urban areas. Since the population is concentrated in urban areas, some growth can already reduce poverty considerably, in particular if accompanied by a pro-poor distributional shift, as in the Doha scenario. Our analyses show that anti-poor changes in the distribution can easily dwarf the poverty reducing potential of growth. The income growth pattern under full liberalization tends to favor poor groups. Poor agricultural and less educated households benefit considerably more from full liberalization than from the Doha liberalizations.

4.5. Conclusions

Our analysis suggests that the economic effects of the Doha round, even of an "optimistic deep" liberalization scenario, are rather limited for Brazil. Accordingly, poverty would remain largely unaffected by this trade reform, which does not appear to be biased in favor any of particularly poor groups. Yet, through a slight improvement in the urban income distribution the Doha scenario has some positive effect on poverty.

In contrast, a full liberalization scenario implies quite substantial welfare gains that are concentrated among some of the poorest groups of the country, in particular those in agriculture. Consequently, the rural poor and certain comparably poor regions in Brazil benefit more than proportionately. This result is driven by an export boom in agriculture and agricultural processing industries, growing labor demand and associated higher wages. Following full liberalization, a smaller number of workers remain in agriculture compared to the BaU. Given that inter sectoral migration may substantially improve the income situation of a household, one may expect full liberalization to weaken poverty reduction. This expectation is supported by the observation that moving households are on average poorer than those remaining in agriculture. However, this is not the case, as the gain in agricultural incomes overcompensates the reduced benefits from lower migration flows.

The beneficial impact of the full liberalization is not limited to rural areas and agricultural activities. The urban poor benefit through higher incomes for unskilled labor also in non-agricultural sectors, which induces a pro-poor shift in the urban income distribution. In addition, the urban poor benefit indirectly from the gains in agriculture, as the pressure on non-agricultural unskilled is relieved somewhat. Trade reform, and in particular domestic trade reforms, may particularly help the Brazilian poor farmers, but only broad-based high growth will eradicate urban poverty.

Whether trade can do the job of significantly raising the incomes of the urban poor is questionable. In this regard an important limitation of our analysis is that we do not assume any dynamic gains from trade liberalization. Our results might hence be taken as a lower bound of the welfare effects, as there is strong evidence of a beneficial impact of trade liberalization on productivity (Winters, McCulloch, and McKay 2004). We also acknowledge that our representation of urban labor markets may be too simple to evaluate the precise effects on some particularly poor groups in urban areas, e.g. in informal activities.

The trade policy implications for Brazil are clear-cut. As Brazil does not lose from the possible Doha scenarios and even slightly gains, there is no reason to oppose such an outcome of the negotiations. Furthermore, our analysis suggests that Brazil and especially the Brazilian poor can substantially gain from own liberalization. An obvious complementary policy to a trade policy that favors the agricultural sector is to enable poor households to participate in agricultural growth. In the Brazilian context, an important means to do so is to provide access to land.

4.6.   Appendices

4.6.1.   Additional tables

App. Table 4.1: Estimation results, mover-stayer model for heads

Number of obs   =   14365
Wald chi2(6)   =   197.120
Prob > chi2   =   0.000
Pseudo R2   =   0.068
Log pseudo-likelihood = -1495.442

	Coef.	Robust Std. Err.	z	P>|z|	[95% Conf. Interval]	
dedu	0.419	0.278	1.510	0.132	-0.126	0.963
age	-0.044	0.005	-9.490	0.000	-0.053	-0.035
ddworkown	-1.123	0.319	-3.520	0.000	-1.749	-0.497
dcess	-0.825	0.327	-2.530	0.012	-1.466	-0.185
dprop	-0.736	0.172	-4.280	0.000	-1.074	-0.399
dgregio1	0.593	0.202	2.930	0.003	0.196	0.990
_cons	-1.708	0.178	-9.580	0.000	-2.058	-1.359

Changes in Predicted Probabilities for Moving out of Agriculture

	0->1	-+sd/2	MargEfct
dedu	0.008		0.007
age		-0.011	-0.001
ddworkown	-0.012		-0.018
dcess	-0.009		-0.013
dprop	-0.010		-0.012
dgregio1	0.012		0.009

Source: Authors' calculations.

Note:
dedu: educational dummy for 10 or more years of schooling
ddworkown: dummy for own-consumption workers
dcess: holding ceded land
dprop: holding own land
dgregio1:   north.

App. Table 4.2: Estimation results, mover-stayer model for non-heads

Number of obs   =   16737
Wald chi2(6)   =   293.58
Prob > chi2   =   0.000
Pseudo R2   =   0.152
Log pseudo-likelihood = -1282.4805

	Coef.	Robust Std. Err.	z	P>|z|	[95% Conf. Interval]	
dprim3	0.782	0.229	3.410	0.001	0.332	1.232
dsec1	0.633	0.298	2.120	0.034	0.049	1.218
dsec2	0.597	0.324	1.840	0.066	-0.039	1.232
exp	0.101	0.023	4.340	0.000	0.055	0.146
exp2	-0.002	0.000	-4.270	0.000	-0.003	-0.001
gend	-0.759	0.188	-4.030	0.000	-1.127	-0.390
preta	-0.500	0.336	-1.490	0.137	-1.159	0.159
ddnonrem	-0.849	0.171	-4.960	0.000	-1.185	-0.513
ddworkown	-1.731	0.307	-5.640	0.000	-2.332	-1.130
dprop	-1.839	0.462	-3.980	0.000	-2.745	-0.934
headnagr	1.122	0.167	6.710	0.000	0.794	1.450
headmover	2.468	0.374	6.610	0.000	1.736	3.200
_cons	-4.369	0.298	-14.640	0.000	-4.954	-3.783

Changes in Predicted Probabilities for Moving out of Agriculture

	0->1	-+sd/2	MargEfct
dprim3	0.010		0.007
dsec1	0.007		0.006
dsec2	0.007		0.005
exp		0.017	0.001
exp2		-0.024	0.000
gend	-0.007		-0.007
preta	-0.004		-0.004
ddnonrem	-0.007		-0.007
ddworkown	-0.011		-0.015
dprop	-0.008		-0.016
headnagr	0.015		0.010
headmover	0.084		0.021

Source: Authors' calculations.

Note:

dprim3:	9 years of schooling	ddnonrem:	non-remunerated household member
dsec1:	11 or 11 years of schooling	ddworkown:	own-consumption worker
dsec2:	12 years of schooling	dprop:	holding own land
exp:	age minus schooling	headnagr:	household head in non-agricultural sector
exp2:	experience squared		
gend:	female	headmover:	head has moved out of agriculture.
preta:	black		

App. Table 4.3: Estimation results, wage/profit equations

Wage/profit equation for agriculture unskilled

Number of obs	=	22699
F(11, 3209)	=	419.53
Prob > F	=	0.000
R-squared	=	0.3021
Root MSE	=	0.83187

	Coef.	Robust Std. Err.	t	P>|t|	[95% Conf. Interval]	
edu	0.084	0.003	27.270	0.000	0.078	0.090
exp	0.047	0.002	29.900	0.000	0.044	0.050
exp2	-0.001	0.000	-28.780	0.000	-0.001	-0.001
gend	-0.858	0.018	-46.640	0.000	-0.894	-0.822
preta	-0.138	0.027	-5.050	0.000	-0.191	-0.084
parda	-0.171	0.016	-10.490	0.000	-0.203	-0.139
nnonrem	0.043	0.009	4.790	0.000	0.025	0.060
drn	-0.129	0.049	-2.620	0.009	-0.225	-0.032
drne	-0.339	0.025	-13.590	0.000	-0.388	-0.290
drs	0.150	0.032	4.720	0.000	0.088	0.213
drcw	0.225	0.036	6.210	0.000	0.154	0.297
_cons	4.079	0.040	102.470	0.000	4.001	4.157

Wage/profit equation for non-agriculture unskilled

Number of obs	=	96993
F(16, 6514)	=	1710.86
Prob > F	=	0.000
R-squared	=	0.423
Root MSE	=	0.67388

	Coef.	Robust Std. Err.	t	P>|t|	[95% Conf. Interval]	
edu	0.008	0.003	2.840	0.004	0.003	0.014
edu2	0.006	0.000	33.350	0.000	0.006	0.007
exp	0.069	0.001	88.200	0.000	0.068	0.071
exp2	-0.001	0.000	-68.950	0.000	-0.001	-0.001
gend	-0.590	0.006	-102.830	0.000	-0.601	-0.579
preta	-0.148	0.011	-13.460	0.000	-0.169	-0.126
parda	-0.143	0.007	-21.910	0.000	-0.156	-0.130
dun	-0.190	0.013	-15.020	0.000	-0.214	-0.165
drn	-0.501	0.106	-4.710	0.000	-0.709	-0.293
dune	-0.450	0.011	-40.590	0.000	-0.472	-0.428
drne	-0.710	0.033	-21.800	0.000	-0.774	-0.646
drse	-0.229	0.029	-7.960	0.000	-0.286	-0.173
dus	-0.069	0.011	-6.470	0.000	-0.090	-0.048
drs	-0.171	0.029	-5.950	0.000	-0.227	-0.115
ducw	-0.123	0.013	-9.420	0.000	-0.149	-0.098
drcw	-0.383	0.054	-7.040	0.000	-0.490	-0.276
_cons	4.494	0.020	227.760	0.000	4.455	4.533

Wage/profit equation for skilled

Number of obs	=	35696
F(16, 6514)	=	995.20
Prob > F	=	0.000
R-squared	=	0.453
Root MSE	=	0.749

	Coef.	Robust Std. Err.	t	P > |t|	[95% Conf. Interval]	
edu	-0.060	0.007	-9.140	0.000	-0.073	-0.047
edu2	0.009	0.000	30.520	0.000	0.009	0.010
exp	0.063	0.002	39.830	0.000	0.060	0.066
exp2	-0.001	0.000	-22.990	0.000	-0.001	-0.001
gend	-0.515	0.009	-55.410	0.000	-0.533	-0.497
preta	-0.277	0.024	-11.570	0.000	-0.324	-0.230
parda	-0.214	0.011	-18.600	0.000	-0.236	-0.191
dun	-0.153	0.023	-6.760	0.000	-0.198	-0.109
drn	-0.520	0.099	-5.260	0.000	-0.714	-0.326
dune	-0.408	0.018	-22.390	0.000	-0.443	-0.372
drne	-0.796	0.044	-18.130	0.000	-0.882	-0.710
drse	-0.276	0.055	-5.030	0.000	-0.384	-0.169
dus	-0.146	0.017	-8.600	0.000	-0.179	-0.113
drs	-0.317	0.052	-6.030	0.000	-0.419	-0.214
ducw	-0.122	0.023	-5.210	0.000	-0.168	-0.076
drcw	-0.108	0.098	-1.100	0.270	-0.301	0.084
_cons	5.278	0.043	122.680	0.000	5.194	5.363

Source: Authors' calculations.

Note:

edu:	years of schooling
edu2:	edu squared
exp:	age minus schooling
exp2:	experience squared
gend:	female 1
preta:	black
parda:	mixed black
nnonrem:	number of non-remunerated household members
d*:	regional dummies with r (u) for rural (urban), n north, ne northeast, s south, cw center-west.

App. Table 4.4: Estimation results, labor market segmentation

Wage equation for testing segmentation hypothesis (unskilled)

Number of obs	=	119692	R-squared	=	0.5021	
F(47, 7228)	=	1232.3	Root MSE	=	0.68619	
Prob > F	=	0				

	Coef.	Robust Std. Err.	t	P>|t|	[95% Conf. Interval]	
dprim1	0.194	0.007	26.410	0.000	0.179	0.208
dprim2	0.343	0.008	41.420	0.000	0.327	0.359
dprim3	0.540	0.010	55.020	0.000	0.521	0.560
dsec1	0.637	0.012	53.890	0.000	0.613	0.660
dsec2	0.878	0.011	81.940	0.000	0.857	0.899
dter	1.464	0.019	78.220	0.000	1.428	1.501
exp	0.058	0.001	83.820	0.000	0.056	0.059
exp2	-0.001	0.000	-69.420	0.000	-0.001	-0.001
d1	*-0.469*	*0.028*	*-16.510*	*0.000*	*-0.524*	*-0.413*
d2	*0.063*	*0.056*	*1.140*	*0.256*	*-0.046*	*0.172*
d3	*-0.011*	*0.024*	*-0.470*	*0.640*	*-0.059*	*0.036*
d4	*-0.238*	*0.017*	*-13.710*	*0.000*	*-0.272*	*-0.204*
d5	*-0.070*	*0.017*	*-4.030*	*0.000*	*-0.104*	*-0.036*
d6	*-0.722*	*0.028*	*-26.200*	*0.000*	*-0.776*	*-0.668*
d7	0.226	0.049	4.610	0.000	0.130	0.322
d8	-0.033	0.012	-2.700	0.007	-0.058	-0.009
d9	0.024	0.016	1.530	0.126	-0.007	0.055
d10	0.020	0.023	0.890	0.374	-0.024	0.065
d11	0.124	0.019	6.520	0.000	0.087	0.162
d12	0.049	0.013	3.880	0.000	0.024	0.074
d13	0.135	0.015	9.230	0.000	0.106	0.164
d15	0.077	0.009	8.540	0.000	0.059	0.094
d16	0.093	0.007	13.020	0.000	0.079	0.107
d17	0.208	0.012	18.080	0.000	0.186	0.231
carteira	0.330	0.006	57.810	0.000	0.318	0.341
seasonal	-0.125	0.017	-7.260	0.000	-0.158	-0.091
dse	0.088	0.009	9.660	0.000	0.070	0.106
arrend	0.116	0.043	2.720	0.007	0.032	0.200
poss	-0.148	0.055	-2.720	0.007	-0.255	-0.041
cess	-0.278	0.041	-6.760	0.000	-0.359	-0.198
prop	0.077	0.023	3.350	0.001	0.032	0.122
dworkown	-0.138	0.021	-6.670	0.000	-0.179	-0.097
nnonrem	0.037	0.007	5.570	0.000	0.024	0.050
gend	-0.531	0.006	-89.070	0.000	-0.542	-0.519
preta	-0.144	0.010	-14.800	0.000	-0.163	-0.125
amarela	0.310	0.054	5.740	0.000	0.204	0.415
parda	-0.135	0.006	-22.770	0.000	-0.147	-0.124
dun	-0.144	0.012	-12.120	0.000	-0.167	-0.120
drn	-0.312	0.044	-7.010	0.000	-0.399	-0.225
dune	-0.422	0.010	-40.210	0.000	-0.443	-0.401
drne	-0.573	0.020	-29.350	0.000	-0.611	-0.534
drse	-0.223	0.021	-10.730	0.000	-0.264	-0.182
dus	-0.081	0.010	-7.960	0.000	-0.101	-0.061
drs	-0.142	0.024	-6.000	0.000	-0.188	-0.095
ducw	-0.081	0.013	-6.460	0.000	-0.105	-0.056
drcw	-0.141	0.026	-5.350	0.000	-0.193	-0.089
isourban2	-0.081	0.049	-1.660	0.098	-0.178	0.015
_cons	4.461	0.017	269.920	0.000	4.429	4.493

Wage equation for testing segmentation hypothesis (skilled)

Number of obs	=		35696	R-squared	=	0.4503
F(47, 7228)	=		357.69	Root MSE	=	0.75121
Prob > F	=		0			

	Coef.	Robust Std. Err.	t	P>|t|	[95% Conf. Interval]	
dprim1	0.200	0.040	5.050	0.000	0.122	0.277
dprim2	0.239	0.038	6.290	0.000	0.165	0.314
dprim3	0.425	0.037	11.490	0.000	0.352	0.497
dsec1	0.490	0.037	13.140	0.000	0.417	0.563
dsec2	0.766	0.035	22.190	0.000	0.698	0.834
dter	1.484	0.036	41.620	0.000	1.414	1.554
exp	0.067	0.002	43.160	0.000	0.064	0.070
exp2	-0.001	0.000	-26.140	0.000	-0.001	-0.001
d1	*-0.417*	*0.152*	*-2.740*	*0.006*	*-0.714*	*-0.119*
d2	*0.499*	*0.176*	*2.840*	*0.005*	*0.154*	*0.843*
d3	*0.216*	*0.211*	*1.020*	*0.306*	*-0.198*	*0.630*
d4	*-0.319*	*0.065*	*-4.870*	*0.000*	*-0.447*	*-0.190*
d5	*0.035*	*0.052*	*0.690*	*0.493*	*-0.066*	*0.136*
d6	*-0.048*	*0.183*	*-0.260*	*0.792*	*-0.407*	*0.311*
d7	0.345	0.073	4.720	0.000	0.202	0.489
d8	0.195	0.033	5.970	0.000	0.131	0.259
d9	0.133	0.037	3.630	0.000	0.061	0.205
d10	0.214	0.035	6.140	0.000	0.146	0.282
d11	0.280	0.036	7.670	0.000	0.208	0.351
d12	0.135	0.034	3.940	0.000	0.068	0.203
d13	0.066	0.034	1.980	0.048	0.001	0.132
d15	0.264	0.031	8.630	0.000	0.204	0.324
d16	0.185	0.015	12.670	0.000	0.157	0.214
d17	0.110	0.015	7.260	0.000	0.081	0.140
carteira	-0.059	0.012	-4.940	0.000	-0.083	-0.036
seasonal	-0.705	0.213	-3.320	0.001	-1.122	-0.289
dse	-0.254	0.025	-10.000	0.000	-0.304	-0.204
arrend	0.627	0.191	3.280	0.001	0.252	1.002
poss	-0.085	0.341	-0.250	0.802	-0.754	0.583
cess	-0.014	0.230	-0.060	0.952	-0.465	0.437
prop	0.391	0.062	6.350	0.000	0.270	0.512
nnonrem	0.039	0.017	2.340	0.019	0.006	0.072
gend	-0.473	0.009	-50.400	0.000	-0.492	-0.455
preta	-0.257	0.024	-10.910	0.000	-0.303	-0.211
amarela	0.255	0.069	3.680	0.000	0.120	0.391
parda	-0.209	0.011	-18.640	0.000	-0.231	-0.187
dun	-0.168	0.022	-7.470	0.000	-0.212	-0.124
drn	-0.635	0.102	-6.230	0.000	-0.835	-0.436
dune	-0.396	0.018	-21.520	0.000	-0.432	-0.360
drne	-0.784	0.040	-19.360	0.000	-0.863	-0.704
drse	-0.368	0.055	-6.730	0.000	-0.475	-0.261
dus	-0.161	0.017	-9.470	0.000	-0.194	-0.127
drs	-0.414	0.055	-7.580	0.000	-0.521	-0.307
ducw	-0.153	0.023	-6.510	0.000	-0.199	-0.107
drcw	-0.224	0.096	-2.330	0.020	-0.413	-0.035
isourban2	-0.028	0.078	-0.360	0.723	-0.180	0.125
_cons	5.007	0.040	123.880	0.000	4.928	5.086

Source: Authors' calculations.
Note: The rows in italics indicates agricultural sectors.

App. Table 4.5: Regional Poverty lines, in 2001 R$

North	Urban	87
	Rural	76
Northeast	Urban	85
	Rural	75
Center-West	Urban	70
	Rural	62
	Distrito Federal	82
Southeast	Urban Rio de Janeiro	80
	Rural Rio de Janeiro	72
	Urban Sao Paulo	84
	Rural Sao Paulo	69
	Urban Minas Gerais and Espirito Santo	66
	Rural Minas Gerais and Espirito Santo	57
South	Urban	83
	Rural	75

Source: Authors' calculations based on Paes de Barros (2004).

App. Table 4.6: Model-GTAP sector mapping

Model Sectors	GTAP 5 Sectors							
CerealGrains	PDR	WHT	GRO					
OilSeeds	OSD							
RawSugar	C_B							
OthCrops	V_F	PFB	OCR	WOL	FRS	FSH		
Livestock	CTL							
RawAnimalProducts	OAP	RMK						
OilMinerals	COL	OIL	GAS	OMN				
LightManufacturing	CMT	MIL	PCR	TEX	WAP			
AgriIndustriesExp	OMT	VOL	SGR	OFD	LEA	B_T		
WoodProductsPaper	LUM	PPP						
ChemicalsOilPr	P_C	CRP						
MetalMineralProducts	NMM	I_S	NFM	FMP				
MachineryEquipment	MVH	ELE	OME	OTN	OMF			
OtherServices	GDT	WTR	ELY	OFI	ISR	OBS	ROS	DWE
Construction	CNS							
TradeCommunication	TRD	CMN	OTP	WTP	ATP			
PublicServices	OSG							

App. Table 4.7: GTAP sector labels

GTAP 5 Sectors

PDR	Paddy rice	LUM	Wood products
WHT	Wheat	PPP	Paper products, publishing
GRO	Cereal grains nec	P_C	Petroleum, coal products
V_F	Vegetables, fruit, nuts	CRP	Chemical, rubber, plastic products
OSD	Oil seeds	NMM	Mineral products nec
C_B	Sugar cane, sugar beet	I_S	Ferrous metals
PFB	Plant-based fibers	NFM	Metals nec
OCR	Crops nec	FMP	Metal products
CTL	Bovine cattle, sheep and goats, horses	MVH	Motor vehicles and parts
OAP	Animal products nec	OTN	Transport equipment nec
RMK	Raw milk	ELE	Electronic equipment
WOL	Wool, silk-worm cocoons	OME	Machinery and equipment nec
FOR	Forestry	OMF	Manufactures nec
FSH	Fishing	ELY	Electricity
COL	Coal	GDT	Gas manufacture, distribution
OIL	Oil	WTR	Water
GAS	Gas	CNS	Construction
OMN	Minerals nec	TRD	Trade
CMT	Bovine meat products	OTP	Transport nec
OMT	Meat products nec	WTP	Water transport
VOL	Vegetable oils and fats	ATP	Air transport
MIL	Dairy products	CMN	Communication
PCR	Processed rice	OFI	Financial services nec
SGR	Sugar	ISR	Insurance
OFD	Food products nec	OBS	Business services nec
B_T	Beverages and tobacco products	ROS	Recreational and other services
TEX	Textiles	OSG	Public Administration, Defense, Education, Health
WAP	Wearing apparel	DWE	Dwellings
LEA	Leather products		

5.   Conclusions, policy relevance, and future research

The main message of the country studies included in this dissertation is that the poverty and distributional impact of external shocks and economic policies depends very much on the exact nature of the shock as well as the structural characteristics of the country in question. Hence, there are no policy blueprints. This may sound trivial, but often enough have policy prescription been based on oversimplifying assumptions without taking into account country-specificities. One such case is the belief that the poor in developing countries in general would benefit from trade liberalization through increased demand for unskilled labor.[105] The Colombian and the Brazilian case studies very well illustrate that the impact of trade liberalization on poverty and the distribution of income depends on the structure of protection in place and how it is modified, i.e. the nature of shock, as well as a number of country characteristics, in particular the functioning of the labor market and the sectoral and skill composition of the workforce. In sum, the studies demonstrate that country-specific empirical research can provide policy-makers with insightful analyses to take better-informed decisions.

Of course, three country-studies cannot provide the empirical basis, on which to judge whether globalization, or some of its many facets, are good or bad for the poor. The analyses may however suffice for the general tentative conclusion that globalization, at least in the Latin American context, is neither good nor bad; rather it entails threats and opportunities. In addition, what appears to be a threat at first sight may actually be seen as an opportunity, given the right policy.

Trade liberalization in Colombia, for example, has increased inequality through a rising wage gap between the skilled and the unskilled. If educational policies however allow labor supply to adjust to this increase, productivity gains would be distributed more equally. The case for better policies to make a difference is even stronger in natural resource abundant countries, in particular during boom phases, as illustrated by the Bolivian study. In the latter, current public expenditure policies were even found to aggravate negative side-effects of the resource boom. A worrying tendency, to which there is no obvious policy response, is the increase in informal employment that is identified in both the Bolivian and the Colombian case. If the informal sector involves negative externalities, for example in terms of human capital accumulation, this increase can harm long-term development prospects.

A fairer world trading system is been by many as an important component of a comprehensive development strategy, as reflected by the adopting the attainment of an "open trading and financial system that is rule-based, predictable and non-discriminatory" committed to "good governance, development and poverty reduction as one of the Millennium Development targets. Even non-governmental

---

105 The structural adjustment programs of the 1980s and early 1990s are another case of fairly similar policy packages applied to a number of countries, whose problems only appeared to be the same at first sight. For a critical view on these programs see Collier and Gunning (1999).

organizations seem to put great hopes in particular into the effects of cutting-down agricultural subsidies in rich countries. For Brazil however, the preceding chapter suggests that the gains for the poor from a new development-and-poverty-focused round of multilateral trade negotiations would be rather limited. This finding is not limited to the Brazilian case. The other country studies included in Hertel and Winters (2005) also point to moderate effects of a "Doha Development Agenda". In some countries, poverty even increases slightly. Among the reasons why liberalizing agricultural trade does not help the poor as much as expected is that, in some countries, higher world market prices are not transmitted to poor farmers, while urban households suffer from the price increase.[106] Such findings again demonstrate that the poverty and distributional impact of economic policies depends on a whole range of country-specific factors and that assessing these effects requires very disaggregated analyses.

In terms of methodology, the chapters demonstrate that the "two-step" or sequential approach provides an appropriate framework to link policies or external shocks to poverty and distributional outcomes. This approach first analyzes the impact of shocks on "distributional drivers", such as changes in prices and factor remunerations, as well as employment shifts between different types of activities or sectors. Using a CGE model in this first stage, allows for a detailed analysis of the transmission channels of the shocks at the "macro" level. In the second step, the final distributional outcome is assessed using a microsimulation model that takes into account the complexities of the income generation process through modelling individual decisions.

The sequential approach brings together two strands of literature, applied CGE models, on the one hand, and poverty and distributional analyses, on the other, which were largely separated from each other. While CGE analyses tend to suffer from being too stylized and not being well informed by micro data, poverty and distributional analyses are often merely descriptive and lack an assessment of the causes of distributional change and the related transmission channels. The sequential approach attempts to get the best out of these two "modeling worlds". Its main advantage is that while it remains tractable both at the macro and the micro level, it allows for sufficiently detailed and disaggregated analyses.

The microsimulation models based on household income generation models provide a powerful tool to assess the final distributional impact of changes in "distributional drivers", as illustrated by the validation exercise in the Colombian chapter. Modeling decisions at the individual level implies that household heterogeneity is not only represented in terms of factor endowments and consumption patterns. The welfare implications of discrete changes in individual behavior, such as labor market entry or sectoral movements, can thus be taken into account. The impact of individual transitions out of agriculture in the Brazil study demonstrates the possible magnitude of these discrete individual changes on

---

106 This is shown by Nicita (2005) for Mexico as well as Arndt et al. (2005) for Mozambique.

household welfare. Here lies the major advantage of such microsimulation models vis-à-vis traditional CGE analyses based on representative household groups.

The shortcomings of the income generation models are discussed at length in each of the chapters and only one major problem should be reconsidered here. It concerns the simulation of occupational transition based on state comparisons. The income generation models for Colombia and Bolivia implicitly assume that the estimated propensity to have a certain occupational status, i.e. to be inactive, or to be employed in the informal/formal or agricultural/non-agricultural sector, is closely related to the propensity to change occupational status. Whether this assumption holds true is an empirical question, which could (and possibly should) be addressed using panel datasets. The Brazilian model relies on employment histories and therefore avoids this problem, but the type of information used reflects to a certain extent short-term behavior.

The Brazilian and the Bolivian chapter use CGE models to trace the transmission channels and quantify the magnitude of the effects of the respective shock. Although widely applied, these models have been criticized for a number of reasons. Analytically, most CGE models rely on the neoclassical framework, although the influence of the "structuralist" school (Taylor 1990) has led to the incorporation of a number of structural characteristics and rigidities in most developing country applications. Which structural characteristics to consider and how to precisely model rigidities, e.g. on factor markets, hence differs between country applications and the research question at hand. The models in this dissertation make an attempt to capture in a realistic way some country characteristics that are key for understanding the transmission of the respective shock. This includes for example the modeling of the gas sector and the related investment flows in the Bolivian model as well as the labor market segmentation in the Brazilian model. Clearly, the two models have their shortcomings. Assuming, for example, neoclassical price setting in the case of traditional agriculture in the Bolivian model, is at best a very rough approximation of reality. In fact, modeling of the rural sector is unsatisfactory in most applied CGE models. Disaggregated input-output data for agriculture are typically not available and agricultural surveys suffer from a lot of problems related to measurement, seasonality, and temporary shocks. In addition to data gaps, the insights from agricultural household models regarding non-separability of production and consumption decisions in rural households (Singh et al. 1986) have not yet entered standard models.[107] More research effort also needs to be dedicated to modeling the informal urban sector. Its heterogeneity in terms of technology, import penetration, and export orientation needs to be addressed. This implies to incorporate the knowledge on the linkages between formal and informal activities into applied

---

[107] See Löfgren and Robinson (1999), who integrate a rural household model into a standard CGE model, for an exception.

models.[108] However, even with all these improvements, eventually the results of a CGE model will be driven by the assumptions made.[109]

Econometricians challenge the empirical relevance of applied CGE models on grounds of the calibration technique based on very restricted functional forms, typically (nested) CES functions. McKitrick (1998) shows the choice of the functional form to make a considerable difference in the results. Yet, in the developing country context, data to estimate these functions is typically not available and the calibration approach overcomes these data restrictions. Furthermore, it is well known that model results are very sensitive to the assumed trade and production elasticities. Harrison et al. (1993) therefore suggest to perform systematic sensitivity analyses and to provide confidence intervals for the results. The CGE analyses in this dissertation, as most CGE model applications, perhaps do too little sensitivity analysis and rely too much on parameters "typically assumed in the literature".

Yet, an assessment of the validity of CGE model results also depends on the purpose of the model. If the analysis is expected to provide a precise numerical estimate of the effects of a specific policy change, the above criticisms have to be taken very seriously. In contrast, if CGE models are seen as a rather stylized, yet empirically underpinned, analytical tool to better understand the transmission channels of a shock through counterfactual analysis and approximate their relative importance, the critique is less relevant. In this dissertation, CGE models are considered such a tool. This is not to say that the numbers resulting from CGE models are without meaning. They should be taken as the results of a model, given a specific set of assumptions. Claiming that CGE modeling experiments would yield "real world forecasts" appears to be exaggerated.[110]

Instead of using a CGE model, the Colombian study relies on secondary sources and additional descriptive analyses to construct the counterfactual scenarios of "distributional drivers" that can be linked to trade reform.[111] Linking ex-post econometric studies on the impact of policies or shocks on "distributional

---

108 See Grimm and Günther (2006) for a recent study on formal-informal linkages in Burkina Faso and a short literature review.

109 See de Maio et el. (1999) and the reply by Sahn et al. (1999) for an exemplary discussion on specific aspects of CGE models applied to developing countries. These aspects include the macroeconomic and labor market closures as well as the assumption on price setting mechanisms. De Maio et al. (1999) challenge the results of a study by Sahn et al. (1997) on the poverty impacts of structural adjustment in Sub-Saharan Africa as reflecting only the assumptions made in the CGE models, and not reality.

110 Admittedly, the CGE applications in this dissertation, in particular the Brazilian chapter, sometimes tend to treat the numbers as being "forecasts".

111 A similar approach is followed by Nicita (2005) who uses his results on price transmission of changes in world market prices in Mexico to simulate the possible effects of trade liberalization on household welfare based on a simple income generation model.

drivers", such wages or prices, to household income generation models seems to be a promising approach for future research. Quite some studies have examined e.g. the impact of trade liberalization on the distribution of wages and employment.[112] The micro analyses in this dissertation have demonstrated that looking at the impact on wages and employment alone does not say much about final distributional outcomes. Increasing female labor market participation provides an example for the complex relationships between employment and wages, on the one hand, and the changes in the distribution of per capita incomes, on the other. Labor market entry of females from poorer households typically worsens the distribution of wages, but may improve welfare of those poorer households considerably. Of course, identifying the effects of a specific shock ex-post is not trivial and requires data with the variation across sectors, regions, and/or time that allows for doing so.

The approach of the Colombian chapter basically combines two "reduced-form" models; a reduced-form model that links trade and labor market outcomes, and a second one that links labor market outcomes and household income. Therefore the exact pathways through which the shocks affect distributional outcomes remain unclear and counterfactual experiments cannot be conducted in such a framework. This would be possible in a general equilibrium model that incorporates heterogeneous individuals. As argued in the introduction, building such an applied model based on a "full-blown, micro-based general equilibrium theory of income distribution and income inequality"[113] does not seem to be feasible for developing countries.

Eventually, the appropriate methodology will depend on the shock or policy to be examined and the data available. Data availability and quality is of central importance to measuring progress towards the Millennium Development goals and to the type of analysis conducted in this dissertation. Applying macro and micro simulation models implies working with different types of data sources including national accounts and primary surveys. The experiences gathered during this research hints at large systematic discrepancies between these different sources. As building Social Accounting Matrices for distributional analysis requires the use of household survey data, applied CGE modelers have also noted the considerable inconsistencies between the two data sources (Round 2003, Robilliard and Robinson 2003). The remainder of this conclusion therefore argues in favor of taking data issues much more seriously and putting them at the heart of the research agenda in development economics.

Deaton (2005) illustrates the scope of the problem. Consumption estimated from surveys is typically lower than consumption from the national accounts by approximately 20 percent, with regional differences. Survey income is on average less than 60 percent of GDP. More worrying than these static comparisons are the differences in growth rates. According to the surveys, average annual real per

---

112 See Arbache et al. (2004) and Winters et al. (2004) for reviews.
113 Quote from James Heckman on the back cover of Bourguignon et al. (2005).

capita consumption growth in the 1990s has been 2.3 percent if the simple average is computed and 1.9 percent if log growth rates are regressed on a time trend. National accounts give growth rates of 3.8 and 4.5 percent, respectively (Deaton 2005). Even if the distribution remains unchanged, consumption growth as measured by the surveys would be too sluggish to make a dent in poverty reduction, while growth measured by national accounts would reduce poverty substantially.

Deaton (2005) provides a discussion of the reasons behind the discrepancies and points to differences that result from differences in definitions, e.g. regarding items to be included into consumption, and differences in meeting those definitions, e.g. in measuring production.[114] National accounts are known to capture production for own consumption, which constitutes an important share of production in poor countries, only to a limited extent. In general, national accounts, in contrast to surveys, are more likely to capture larger transactions than smaller ones (Deaton 2005). As these small transactions are those reflecting the living standards of the poor, Deaton (2005) concludes that poverty can only be measured using household surveys. However, understanding the relationship between growth, inequality and poverty will require a reconciliation of macro and micro data.

In light of these findings, the discipline dedicates astonishingly little effort to data issues. The main problem of basing empirical research on these obviously flawed datasets lies in the fact that the reasons for these differences are likely by to systematic. Yet, as biases are systematic, they can and should be investigated. The described data inconsistencies are not a technical question of interest to insiders, but a key problem when progress towards the Millennium Development Goals needs to be measured: Where is the point of setting quantitative development targets if we lack the means to measure them?

---

114 See also Robilliard and Robinson (2003) and Ravallion (2001b).

6. References

Adelman, I. and C.T. Morris (1973). *Economic Growth and Social Equity in Developing Countries*. Stanford: Stanford University Press.

Adelman I. and S. Robinson (1978). *Income Distribution Policy in Developing Countries: A Case Study of Korea*. New York: Oxford University Press.

Adelman, I. and S. Robinson (1989). Income Distribution and Development. In: Chenery, H. and T.N. Srinivasan (eds.). *Handbook of Development Economics Volume II*. Amsterdam: North Holland, pp. 949-1004.

Aghion, P., E. Caroli, and C. Garcia-Penalosa. (1999). Inequality and Economic Growth: The Perspective of the New Growth Theories. *Journal of Economic Literature*, 37 (4), pp. 1615-1660.

Alatas, V. and F. Bourguignon (2005). The Evolution of Income Distribution during Indonesia's fast Growth, 1980-96. In: Bourguignon, F., F.H.G. Ferreira, and N. Lustig (eds.). *The Microeconomics of Income Distribution Dynamics*. Washington, D.C.: The World Bank and Oxford University Press.

Anand, S. (1983). *Inequality and Poverty in Malaysia*. Oxford: Oxford University Press.

Arndt, C. (2005). The Doha Round and Mozambique. In: Hertel, T. and L. A. Winters (2005*)*. *Poverty and the WTO. Impacts of the Doha Development Agenda*. Washington D.C.: Palgrave and The World Bank.

Arbache, J.S., A. Dickerson, and F. Green (2004). Trade Liberalisation and Wages in Developing Countries. *Economic Journal*, 114 (493), pp. F73-96.

Armington, P.S. (1969). A Theory of Demand for Products Distinguished by Place of Production. *IMF Staff Papers*, 16, pp. 159-178.

Atkinson, A. and F. Bourguignon (2000). Income Distribution and Economics. In Atkinson, A. and F. Bourguignon, (eds.). *Handbook of Income Distribution*, Vol. 1, Amsterdam: North-Holland, pp. 1-58.

Attanasio, O., P. Goldberg, and N. Pavcnik (2004). Trade Reforms and Wage Inequality in Colombia. *Journal of Development Economics*, 74 (2), pp. 331-366.

Auty, R.M. (ed.) (2001). *Resource Abundance and Economic Development*. Oxford: Oxford University Press.

Auty, R.M. and J.L. Evia (2001). A Growth Collapse with Point Resources: Bolivia. In: Auty, R.M. (ed.). *Resource Abundance and Economic Development*. Oxford: Oxford University Press.

Barrett, C.B. (2004). Rural Poverty Dynamics: Development Policy Implications. Paper prepared for invited presentation at the 25th International Conference of Agricultural Economists, Durban, South Africa.

Blinder, A.S. (1973). Wage Discrimination: Reduced Form and Structural Estimates. *Journal of Human Resources* 8 (4), pp. 436-455.

Bourguignon, F., F.H.G. Ferreira, and P.G. Leite (2002). Ex-ante Evaluation of Conditional Cash Transfer Programs: The Case of Bolsa Escola. World Bank Policy Research Working Paper No. 2916.

Bourguignon, F. and F.H.G. Ferreira (2005). Decomposing Changes in the Distribution of Household Incomes: Methodological Aspects. In: Bourguignon, F., F.H.G. Ferreira, N. Lustig (eds.). *The Microeconomics of Income Distribution Dynamics.* Washington, D.C.: The World Bank and Oxford University Press.

Bourguignon F., M. Fournier, and M. Gurgand (1998). Wage and Labor Force Participation Behavior in Taiwan, 1979-1994. Mimeo.

Bourguignon F., M. Fournier, and M. Gurgand (2001). Fast Development with a Stable Income Distribution:Taiwan, 1979-1994. *Review of Income and Wealth,* 47 (2), pp. 139-163.

Bourguignon, F., A.-S. Robilliard, and S. Robinson (2005). Representative vs. Real Households in the Macroeconomic Modeling of Inequality. In: Kehoe, T.J., T.N. Srinivasan, and J. Whalley (eds.). Frontiers in Applied General Equilibrium Modeling. Cambridge: Cambridge University Press.

Bourguignon, F., F.H.G. Ferreira, and N. Lustig (eds.) (2005a). *The Microeconomics of Income Distribution Dynamics.* Washington, D.C.: The World Bank and Oxford University Press.

Bourguignon, F., F.H.G. Ferreira, and N. Lustig (2005b). A Synthesis of the Results. In: F. Bourguignon, F.H.G. Ferreira, and N. Lustig (eds.) (2005). *The Microeconomics of Income Distribution Dynamics.* Washington, D.C.: The World Bank and Oxford University Press.

Bourguignon, F., J. de Melo, J. and C. Morrisson (1991) Poverty and Income Distribution During Adjustment. *World Development,* 19 (11), pp. 1485-1508.

Bussolo, M., and J. Lay (2005). Globalisation and Poverty Changes in Colombia. In: Bussolo, M. and J. Round (eds.). *Globalisation and Poverty - Channels and Policy Responses.* London: Routledge.

Chenery, H., M. Ahluwalia, C. Bell, J. Duloy, and R. Jolly (1974). *Redistribution with Growth.* Oxford: Oxford University Press.

Christiaensen, L., L. Demery, and S. Paternostro (2003). Macro and Micro Perspectives of Growth and Poverty in Africa. *World Bank Economic Review* 17 (3): 317–347.

Cline, W.R. (1975). Distribution and Development. A Survey of the Literature. *Journal of Development Economics,* 1 (4), pp. 359-400.

Cockburn, J. (2006). Trade liberalisation and poverty in Nepal : a computable general equilibrium micro-simulation analysis In: Bussolo, M. and J.R. Round (eds.). *Globalisation and Poverty: Channels and Policy Responses.* London: Routledge., pp. 171-194.

Cogneau, D. (2001). Formation du revenue, segmentation et discrimination sur le marché du travail d'une ville en développement: Antananarivo fin de siècle. DIAL DT/2001/18.

Cogneau, D. and A.S. Robilliard (2001). Growth, Distribution and Poverty in Madagascar: Learning from a Microsimulation Model in a General Equilibrium Framework. TMD Discussion Paper 61. Washington, D.C.: IFPRI.

Collier, P. and W. Gunning (1999). The IMF'S Role in Structural Adjustment. *The Economic Journal*, 109 (459), pp. 634-651.

Collier P. and J.W. Gunning (1999a). *Trade Shocks in Developing Countries. Vol. 1: Africa*. Oxford: Oxford University Press.

Collier P. and J.W. Gunning (1999b). *Trade Shocks in Developing Countries. Vol. 2: Asia and Latin America*. Oxford: Oxford University Press.

Cornia, G., R. Jolly, F. Stewart (1987). *Adjustment with a Human Face*. Oxford: Oxford University Press.

De Maio, L., F. Stewart, and R. van der Hoeven (1999). Computable general equilibrium models, adjustment, and the poor in Africa. *World Development*, 27 (3), pp. 453-470

Deaton, A. (1997). *The Analysis of Household Surveys. A Microeconometric Approach to Development Policy*. Washington D.C.: The World Bank and John Hopkins University Press.

Deaton, A. (2004). Measuring Poverty in a Growing World (or Measuring Growth in a Poor World). *Review of Economics and Statistics*, 87 (1), pp. 1-19.

Dervis, K., J. de Melo, and S. Robinson (1982). General Equilibrium Models for Development Policy. Cambridge: Cambridge University Press.

Dias, G.L.S., C.M. Amaral (2002). Structural Change in Brazilian Agriculture, 1980-98. In: Baumann, R. (2002). *Brazil in the 1990s – An Economy in Transition*. Houndsmill: Palgrave.

Dollar, D. and A. Kraay (2002). Growth *is* Good for the Poor. *Journal of Economic Growth*, 7, pp. 195–225.

Edwards, S. (1998). Openness, Productivity, and Growth. What do we really know? *Economic Journal*, 108 (447), pp. 383-398.

Elbers, C., J.O. Lanjouw, P. Lanjouw, and P.G. Leite (2004). Poverty and Inequality in Brazil: New Estimates from Combined PPV-PNAD Data. The Word Bank. Mimeo.

Escobar, F. and O. Nina (2004). Pension Reform in Bolivia: A Review of Approach and Experience. *Study No. GI-E6*. La Paz: Grupo Integral.

ESMAP (2002). Estudio Comparativo sobre la Distribución de la Renta Petrolera Estudio de Casos: Bolivia, Colombia, Ecuador y Peru. Mimeo.

Falvey, R. and C.D. Kim (1992). Timing and Sequencing Issues in Trade Liberalization. *Economic Journal*, 102 (413), pp. 908-924.

Feenstra, C. and G.H. Hanson (1995). Foreign Direct Investment and Relative Wages: Evidence from Mexico's Maquiladoras. NBER Working Paper No. W5122.

Ferreira, F.H.G. and J. Litchfield (1999). Calm After the Storms: Income Distribution and Welfare in Chile, 1987-1994. *World Bank Economic Review*, 13 (3), pp. 509-538.

Ferreira, H.G.F. and R. Paes de Barros (2005). The Slippery Slope: Explaining the Increase in Extreme Poverty in Urban Brazil, 1976-96. In: F. Bourguignon, F.H.G. Ferreira, and N. Lustig (eds.). *The Microeconomics of Income Distribution Dynamics*. Wasington, D.C.: The World Bank and Oxford University Press.

Ferreira, H.G., P. Lanjouw, and M. Neri (2001). A Robust Poverty Profile for Brazil Using Multiple Data Sources. Paper Presented at the LACEA 2000 and ANPEC 2001 meetings.

Fields, G. (1989). Changes in Poverty and Inequality in Developing Countries. World *Bank Research Observer*, 4 (2), pp. 167-184.

Fiess, N.M. and D. Verner (2003). Migration and Human Capital in Brazil During the 1990s. World Bank Policy Research Working Paper No. 3093.

Gelb, A.H. (1988). *Oil Windfalls: Blessing or Curse?* New York: Oxford University Press.

Golan, A., G. Judge, and D. Miller (1996). *Maximum Entropy Econometrics. Robust Estimation with Limited Data*. Chichester: John Wiley and Sons.

Goldberg, P. and N. Pavcnik (2003). The Response of the Informal Sector to Trade Liberalization. *Journal of Development Economics*, 72 (2), pp. 463-496.

Goldberg, P. and N. Pavcnik (2004a). The Effects of the Colombian Trade Liberalization on Urban Poverty. Paper prepared for the NBER Globalization and Poverty Conference, Cape Cod.

Goldberg, P. and N. Pavcnik (2004b). Trade, Inequality, and Poverty: What Do We Know? Evidence from Recent Trade Liberalization Episodes in Developing Countries. NBER Working Paper No. 10593.

Goldberg, P. and N. Pavcnik (2005). Trade, Wages, and the Political Economy of Trade Protection: Evidence from the Colombian Trade Reforms. *Journal of International Economics*, 66 (1), pp. 75-105.

Grimm, M. (2005), Educational policies and poverty reduction in Côte d'Ivoire. *Journal of Policy Modeling*, 27, pp. 231-247.

Grimm, M. and I. Günther (2006), Inter- and intra-household linkages between the informal and formal sector. A case study for urban Burkina Faso. In: Guha-Khasnobis, B. and R. Kanbur (eds.). *Informal Labor Markets and Development*, London: Palgrave Macmillan.

Grimm, M., S. Klasen, and A. McKay (2006). Determinants of Pro-Poor Growth: Analytical Issues and Findings from Country Cases. London: Palgrave Macmillan, forthcoming.

Harrison, A. (2005). Globalization and Poverty: An NBER Study. University of California at Berkeley and NBER (Draft).

Harrison, G.W., R. Jones, L. J. Kimbell, R. Wigle (1993). How robust is applied general equilibrium analysis? *Journal of Policy Modeling*, 15 (1), pp. 99-115

Harrison, G., Rutherford, T., and Tarr, D. (2000) Trade liberalization, poverty and efficient equity. *Journal of Development Economics* (2003) 71, pp. 97–128.

Harrison, G.W., T.F. Rutherford, D. Tarr, and A. Gurgel (2003). Regional, Multilateral, and Unilateral Trade Policies of MERCOSUR for Growth and Poverty Reduction in Brazil. World Bank Working Paper No. 3051.

Helfand, S.M. and G.C. De Rezende (2004). The Impact of Sector-Specific and Economy-Wide Reforms on the Agricultural Sector in Brazil: 1980-98. *Contemporary Economic Policy*, 22 (2), pp. 194-212.

Hertel, T. and L. A. Winters (2005*). Poverty and the WTO. Impacts of the Doha Development Agenda*. Washington D.C.: Palgrave and The World Bank.

IBGE (Instituto Brasileiro de Geografia e Estatística) (1997). *Anuário Estatístico do Brasil 57*. Rio de Janeiro: Ministério Planejamento e Orçamento.

Jaramillo, C.F. (2001). Liberalization, Crisis, and Change: Colombian Agriculture in the 1990s. *Economic Development and Cultural Change*, 49 (4), pp. 821-846.

Johnston, J. and J. Di Nardo (1997). *Econometric Methods*. 4th ed., New York: McGraw-Hill.

Kanbur, R. (2000). Income Distribution and Development. In: Atkinson, A. and F. Bourguignon, (eds.). *Handbook of Income Distribution*, Vol. 1, Amsterdam: North-Holland, pp. 791-841.

Kappel, R., J. Lay, and S. Steiner (2005). Uganda: No More Pro-Poor Growth? *Development Policy Review*, 23 (1), pp. 27-53.

Klasen, S., M. Grosse, J. Lay, J. Spatz, R. Thiele, and M. Wiebelt (2006). Country Case Study Bolivia. In: Grimm, M., A. McKay, and S. Klasen (eds.). *Determinants of Pro-Poor Growth: Analytical Issues and Findings from 14 country case studies*. London: Palgrave-Macmillan (forthcoming).

Kuznets, S. (1955). Economic growth and income inequality. *American Economic Review*, 45 (1), pp. 1-28.

Lal, D. (1976). Distribution and Development. A Review Article. *World Development*, 4 (9), pp. 725-738.

Lay, J. and T. Omar Mahmoud (2004). Bananas, Oil, and Development: Examining the Resource Curse and Its Transmission Channels by Resource Type. Kiel Working Paper No. 1218.

Lay, J., R. Thiele, and M. Wiebelt (2006). Shocks, Policy Reforms and Pro-poor Growth in Bolivia: A Simulation Analysis. *Review of Development Economics*, forthcoming.

Lewis, W.A. (1954) Economic Development with Unlimited Supplies of Labor. Manchester school of Economics and Social Studies 22, pp. 139-181.

Löfgren, H. and S. Robinson (1999). To Trade or Not To Trade: Non-separable Farm Household Models in Partial and General Equlibrium. TMD Discussion Paper 37, Trade and Macroeconomics Division, Washington, D.C.: International Food Policy Research Institute.

Löfgren, H., R. Lee Harris, S. Robinson (2002). A Standard Computable General Equilibrium (CGE) Model in GAMS. Microcomputers in Policy Research No. 5, International Food Policy Research Institute, Washington, D.C..

Long J.S. and J. Freese (2001). *Regression Models for Categorical Dependent Variables Using STATA*. College Station, Tex.: STATA Press.

Martin, W. and D. Mitra (1999). Productivity Growth and Convergence in Agriculture and Manufacturing. World Bank Policy Research Paper No. 2171.

Martinez, S. (2004). Pensions, Poverty and Household Investments in Bolivia. Mimeo.

McKitrick, R.R. (1998). The Econometric Critique of Computable General Equilibrium Modeling: The Role of Functional Forms. *Economic Modelling*,15 (4), pp. 543-573.

Nakosteen, R.A. and M. Zimmer (1980). Migration and Income: The Question of Self Selection. *Southern Economic Journal*, 46 (3), pp. 840-851.

Nicita, A. (2005). Multilateral Trade Liberalization and Mexican Households: The Effect of the Doha Developments Agenda. In: Hertel, T. and L. A. Winters (2005*). Poverty and the WTO. Impacts of the Doha Development Agenda*. Washington D.C.: Palgrave and The World Bank.

Núñez, J. A. and J.A. Jiménez (1997). Correcciones a los Ingresos de la Encuestas de Hogares y Distribución del Ingreso Urbano en Colombia. República de Colombia, Departamento de Planeación. Mimeo.

Oaxaca, R. (1973). Male-Female Wage Differentials in Urban Labor Markets. *International Economic Review* 14 (3), pp. 693-709.

Ocampo, J.A. (1999). An Ongoing Structural Transformation: The Colombian Economy 1986-1996. In: Taylor, L. (ed.). *After Neoliberalism. What Next for Latin America?* Ann Arbor: University of Michigan Press.

Ocampo, J.A., F. Sánchez, and C.E. Tovar (2000). Mercado Laboral y Distribución del Ingreso en Colombia en los Años Noventa. *Revista de la CEPAL*, 72, pp. 53-78.

Paes de Barros, R. (2004). Pobreza Rural e Trabalho Agrícola no Brasil ao Longo da Década de Noventa. Mimeo.

Ravallion, M. (2001a). Growth, Inequality, and Poverty: Looking beyond the Averages. *World Development*, 29 (11), pp. 1803-1815.

Ravallion, M. (2001b). Should Poverty Measures be Anchored to the National Accounts? *Economic and Political Weekly*, pp. 3245-3252.

Ravallion, M. and Datt, G. (1999). When is Growth Pro-Poor? Evidence from the Diverse Experiences of India's states. World Bank Policy Research Working Paper No. 2263.

Ravallion, M. and S. Chen (2003). Measuring pro-poor growth. *Economics Letters*, 78 (1), pp. 93-99.

Robilliard, A. S. and S. Robinson (2003) Reconciling household surveys and national accounts data using a cross-entropy estimation method *Review of Income and Wealth*, 49(3), pp. 395 - 406.

Robilliard, A.-S., F. Bourguignon, and S. Robinson (2002). Crisis and Income Distribution: A Micro-Macro Model for Indonesia. Mimeo.

Robinson, S. (1989). Multisectoral Models. In: Chenery, H. and T.N. Srinivasan (eds.) (1989). Handbook of Development Economics. Elsevier Science Publishers, pp. 885-947.

Rodriguez, F. and D. Rodrik (2000). Trade Policy and Economic Growth: A Skeptic's Guide to the Cross-National Evidence. In: Bernanke, B. and K.S. Rogoff (eds.). *NBER Macro Annual 2000*. Cambridge, MA: NBER.

Round, J. I. (2003). Constructing SAMs for Development Policy Analysis: Lessons Learned and Challenges Ahead. Economic Systems Research, Vol. 15, No. 2.

Sachs, J.D. and A.M. Warner (1997). Natural Resource Abundance and Economic Growth. Harvard Institute for International Development, Development Discussion Paper No. 517a.

Sahn, D.E. and S.D. Younger (2002). Estimating the Incidence of Indirect Taxes in Developing Countries," Chapter 1 in Evaluating the distributional and poverty effects of macro policies, a compendium of existing techniques: introducing linkages between macro and micro techniques, World Bank online.

Sahn, D.E., P. Dorosh, and S.D. Younger (1997). *Structural Adjustment Reconsidered: Economic Policy and Poverty in Africa*. Cambridge: Cambridge University Press.

Sahn, D.E., P. Dorosh, and S.D. Younger (1999). A reply to De Maio, Stewart, and van der Hoeven. *World Development*, 27 (3), pp. 471-475

Singh, I., L. Squire, and J. Strauss (eds) (1986). *Agricultural Household Models. Extensions, Applications, and Policy*. Baltimore and London: The Johns Hopkins University Press.

Spatz, J. (2004a). The Impact of Structural Reforms on Wages and Employment: The Case of Formal versus Informal Workers in Urban Bolivia. *Latin American Journal of Economic Development* 1 (2), pp. 91-122.

Spatz, J. (2004b). The Impact of Structural Reforms on Wages and Employment: The Case of Formal versus Informal Workers in Urban Bolivia. *Revista Latino Americana de Desarrollo Económico*, 1 (2), pp. 91-122.

Srinivasan, T.N., and J. Bhagwati, (1999), Outward-Orientation and Development: Are Revisionists Right? Yale University. Mimeo.

Tannuri-Pianto, M., D. Pianto, and O. Arias (2004). Informal Employment in Bolivia. A lost Propostion? World Bank Poverty Assessment. Mimeo.

Taubman, P. and M. Wachter (1986). Segmented Labor Markets. In: Ashenfelter, O. and R. Layard (eds.) (1986). *Handbook of Labor Economics. Vol. II*. Amsterdam: North Holland.

Taylor, L. (1990). Structuralist CGE Models. In Taylor, L. (ed.). *Socially Relevant Policy Analysis*. Cambridge, MA: MIT Press.

Train, K. (2003). *Discrete Choice Methods with Simulation*. Cambridge: Cambridge University Press.

UNDP (1998). *Informe de Desarrollo Humano para Colombia 1998*. Santafé de Bogotá: TM Editores.

Van der Mensbrugghe, D. (2003). Prototype Model for Real Computable General Equilibrium Model for the State Development Planning Commission, P. R. China. Mimeo.

Vélez, C. E., J. Leibovich, A. Kugler, C. Bouillón, and J. Núñez (2005), The Reversal of Inequality Trends in Colombia 1978-1995: A Combination of Persistent and Fluctuating Forces. In: Bourguignon, F., F.H.G. Ferreira, and N. Lustig (eds.). *The Microeconomics of Income Distribution Dynamics.* Washington, D.C.: The World Bank and Oxford University Press.

Verner, D. (2004). Making the Poor Count Takes More Than Counting the Poor – A Quick Poverty Assessment of the State of Bahia, Brazil. World Bank Policy Research Working Paper No. 3216.

Wiebelt, M. (1996). *Anpassung und Einkommensverteilung in Entwicklungsländern – Eine angewandte allgemeine Gleichgewichtsanalyse für Malaysia.* Kieler Studien 276, Tübingen: Mohr Siebeck.

Winters, L.A., N. McCulloch, and A. McKay (2004). Trade Liberalization and Poverty: The Evidence So Far. *Journal of Economic Literature*, 42 (1), pp. 72-115.

Wood, A. (1997). Openness and Wage Inequality in Developing Countries: The Latin American Challenge to East Asian Conventional Wisdom. *World Bank Economic Review*, 11 (1), pp. 33-57.

World Bank (2002). *Colombia Poverty Report.* Washington, D.C.: The World Bank.

World Bank (2003). Brazil – Inequality and Economic Development. Vol. 1. Policy Report No. 24487-BR.

World Bank (2004). Bolivia. Public Expenditure Management for Fiscal Sustainability and Equitable and Efficient Public Services. Report No. 28519-BO. Washington, D.C.: The World Bank.

World Bank (2005a). Equity and Development. World Development Report 2006. Washington, D.C.: The World Bank and Oxford University Press.

World Bank (2005b). Pro-poor Growth in the 1990s. Lessons and Insights from 14 Countries. Washington D.C.: The World Bank.

Yanikkaya, H. (2003). Trade Openness and Economic Growth: a Cross-country Empirical Investigation. *Journal of Development Economics*, 72 (1), pp. 57-89.

Göttinger Studien zur Entwicklungsökonomik
Göttingen Studies in Development Economics

Herausgegeben von/Edited by Hermann Sautter
und/and Stephan Klasen

Die Bände 1-8 sind über die Vervuert Verlagsgesellschaft (Frankfurt/M.) zu beziehen.

www.peterlang.de

Mareike Meyn

The Impact of EU Free Trade Agreements on Economic Development and Regional Integration in Southern Africa

The Example of EU-SACU Trade Relations

Frankfurt am Main, Berlin, Bern, Bruxelles, New York, Oxford, Wien, 2006.
453 pp., num. fig. and tab.
Development economics and policy.
Series edited by Franz Heidhues and Joachim von Braun. Vol. 55
ISBN 978-3-631-55354-1 · pb. € 74.50*

North-South Free Trade Agreements are supposed to improve African countries' access to competitive inputs and consumer goods, to assist in creating an enabling trading environment and to help to improve the competitiveness of domestic companies by involving them in international networks. Negative effects such as revenue losses and trade diversion are meant to be offset by safeguard measures, technical assistance, and economic growth. The effects of a free trade agreement between the EU and the Southern African Customs Union (SACU) countries, especially relating to export performance, diversification efforts, industrialisation options and efforts for deeper regional integration, are the major questions the study addresses. In studying sector examples in the SACU countries for successful industrial policy, an investigation is undertaken of how a free trade agreement between the EU and the SACU countries affects domestic policies, economic performance and the position of sectors in the global value chain. The conclusion drawn is that free trade agreements concluded between the EU and southern African countries failed to be development-oriented. Subsequently, policy recommendations are made as to how EU policies towards southern Africa can take industrial development, export diversification and a move towards deeper regional integration better into account.

Frankfurt am Main · Berlin · Bern · Bruxelles · New York · Oxford · Wien
Distribution: Verlag Peter Lang AG
Moosstr. 1, CH-2542 Pieterlen
Telefax 00 41 (0) 32 / 376 17 27

*The €-price includes German tax rate
Prices are subject to change without notice
Homepage http://www.peterlang.de